Do animals have moral rights? In contrast to the philosophical gurus of the animal rights movement, whose opinion has held moral sway in recent years, Peter Carruthers here claims that they do not. *The animals issue* provides an admirably clear discussion of the role theoretical considerations have to play in determining our moral judgement. Carruthers explores a variety of moral theories, exposing the weaknesses of those that would accord rights to animals, and concluding that contractualism (in the tradition of Kant and Rawls) offers the most acceptable framework. From such a perspective animals lack direct moral significance. This need not entail of course that there are no moral constraints on our treatment of them.

This provocative but judiciously argued book is for all those interested in animal rights, whatever their initial standpoint. It will also serve as a lively introduction to ethics, demonstrating why theoretical issues in ethics actually matter.

THE ANIMALS ISSUE

THE ANIMALS ISSUE

Moral theory in practice

PETER CARRUTHERS

Professor of Philosophy, University of Sheffield

CAMBRIDGE
UNIVERSITY PRESS

Published by the Press Syndicate of the University of Cambridge
The Pitt Building, Trumpington Street, Cambridge, CB2 1RP
40 West 20th Street, New York, NY 10011-4211 USA
10 Stamford Road, Oakleigh, Melbourne 3166, Australia

First published 1992
Reprinted 1994

Printed in Great Britain by Athenæum Press Ltd, Newdastle upon Tyne

A catalogue record for this book is available from the British Library

Library of Congress cataloguing in publication data
Carruthers, Peter. 1952–
The animals issue: moral theory in practice / Peter Carruthers.
p.   cm.
Includes index.
ISBN 0 521 43092 5 (hardback). – ISBN 0 521 43689 3 (paperback)
1. Animal rights. 1. Title.
HV4708.c38   1992
179′.3 – dc20   92-9338 CIP

ISBN 0 521 43092 5 hardback
ISBN 0 521 43689 3 paperback

For Daniel
whose animal days are almost done

Contents

Preface

The animal rights movement has gained considerable momentum in recent years, fuelled, in part, by the theoretical arguments of moral philosophers. Indeed, it is striking that almost all of the books and articles recently published on this issue have argued in favour of the moral standing of animals. This is not because the consensus amongst moral philosophers as a whole is that animals have rights. It is rather because, for one reason or another, most of those who take the opposite view have chosen to remain silent. This book is written in an attempt to redress the balance.

My view is that the case for the moral standing of animals is weak, and that the contrary case is, by contrast, very powerful. In fact, I regard the present popular concern with animal rights in our culture as a reflection of moral decadence. Just as Nero fiddled while Rome burned, many in the West agonise over the fate of seal pups and cormorants while human beings elsewhere starve or are enslaved. This reaction is, to a degree, understandable. For animal sufferers are always blameless, and the steps necessary to improve their situation are generally plain. Our response to human suffering, in contrast, is often complicated by the suspicion that the victims, or their political representatives, are at least partially responsible for their fate, and by knowledge of the fearsome complexity of the economic and social problems involved in such issues as famine relief. Whatever may have been true of Nero, our species of decadence may consist in a weakness for easy options, rather than in any failure of moral sensitivity.

The recent explosion of interest in animal rights has had a

variety of sources, no doubt, besides moral paralysis in face of the enormity of the world's human problems. One such source may be the increasing ubanisation of Western culture that has dramatically diminished the extent of personal working contact with animals. The sentimentality that many people feel for their pets has thus come to spread itself over the whole animal domain. But another source has undoubtedly been intellectual. The philosophical gurus of the animal rights movement have managed to seize the moral high ground, charging those who oppose them with inconsistency or morally arbitrary speciesism. The main purpose of this book is to show that these charges can be rebutted. Besides exposing the implausibility of those theories that would grant rights to animals, I shall defend a theoretical framework that accords full moral standing to all human beings, while non-arbitrarily withholding such standing from animals.

In attacking those who attribute moral standing to animals, however, I am not opposing those who are animal *lovers*, as I explain in the opening chapter. Indeed, I count myself as belonging to the latter group. But it is one thing to love animals for their grace, beauty, and marvellous variety, and quite another to believe that they make any direct moral claims upon us. Nor should I be seen as placing myself in opposition to recent ecology movements. But my view is that rare species of animal and rain forests are worth preserving for their importance to *us*, not because they have moral significance, or moral rights, in their own right. Far from being strengthened, the ecology movement is only weakened by association with such extreme and indefensible views.

This book is aimed primarily at non-philosophers, in the sense that I try to take nothing for granted, and lay out my material as clearly and explicitly as I can. All I assume is that my readers are prepared to think while they read, and that they can follow the course of a rational argument. This does not mean, however, that I talk down to my audience. I do not write from any position of specialised knowledge or superior wisdom, but only as one who has tried to think honestly and openly about the issues. In any case, I belong to that breed of contemporary philosopher who holds that the life-blood of philosophy is accessibility. Where philosophy retreats into technicality it withers and dies, and where it takes refuge in obscurity it only forms a rallying point for those who care nothing for truth.

I have two remarks to make about grammar. One is that although human beings are, strictly speaking, a species of animal, for reasons of simplicity I shall use the term 'animal', throughout, in such a way as to contrast with 'human being'. When I therefore raise the question whether any animals have rights, what I am asking, in fact, is whether any non-human animals have rights. My second remark is political. Wherever necessary, I shall use the colloquial plural pronouns 'they' and 'their' in impersonal contexts in place of the pernicious masculine singular 'he' and 'his' required by strict English grammar. For I do not wish to endorse the impression that only men ever do or think anything worth mentioning. I find this option less distracting than the use of the feminine 'she' and 'hers' favoured by some writers. Yet it is less stylistically barbaric than 's/he' and 'his/hers', and less unwieldy than the constant use of 'he or she' and 'his or hers'.

As for my intellectual debts, it was originally through discussions with Clare McCready that I came to feel I had a distinctive approach to the question of animal significance, which might be worth putting down on paper. I am grateful to her for her strident but thoughtful opposition. Thanks also go to the following individuals for their comments and advice on previous drafts: David Archard, Stephen Buckle, Nick Bunnin, Daniel Dennett, Debbie Fitzmaurice, Peter Harrison, Jennifer Jackson, Susan Levi, Stephen Makin, Christopher McKnight, Susan Mendus, Onora O'Neill, Peter Singer, Robert Stern, Robert Wurtz, and an anonymous reader for Cambridge University Press. That I have not acknowledged their individual contributions in the pages that follow does not mean that they are not remembered – only that a text of this sort should be as uncluttered by scholarly apparatus as possible. I am also grateful to my students at the Queen's University, Belfast, and the universities of Michigan, Essex, and Sheffield, on whom I tried out my ideas at various stages of their formation.

Moral argument and moral theory

The task of this book is to consider whether animals have *moral standing* – that is, whether they have rights that we may infringe by killing them or causing them suffering, or whether there is some other way in which we have direct moral duties towards them. In this first chapter I shall lay the foundation for what follows, discussing the role of theoretical considerations within morality and the methods that may be appropriate in resolving moral disputes. I shall also argue that some kinds of moral theory are too implausible to be taken seriously.

THE LIMITS OF MORALITY

It needs to be emphasised that our question about the moral standing of animals is not the same as the question whether animals *matter*. There are many things that matter to us which do not give rise to moral rights or duties (or at least not directly – I shall return to this point shortly). Ancient buildings, oak trees, and works of art matter greatly to many of us without, I think, having moral standing. It is hardly sensible to say that a medieval castle, the oak on the village green, or the *Mona Lisa* have a moral right to be preserved. Nor is it plausible to claim that we have moral duties with respect to these things – though some people may have professional duties to care for them, through their roles as museum curators or foresters.

Things that lack moral standing may nevertheless have indirect moral significance, giving rise to moral duties in a round-about way. Thus, while medieval castles are not the kinds of thing that can have rights, and while we have no moral duties towards them as such, it is plainly of moral significance that many people care deeply about them. This may be sufficient to give rise to duties to preserve and protect. Even the legitimate owner of a medieval castle may be under a moral obligation not to destroy it, since this would deprive present and future generations of a source of wonder, and of attachment to the past. So even if we were to agree that animals lack moral standing, it would not follow that we can, with impunity, treat animals as we please. For there may still be indirect duties towards animals arising out of the legitimate concerns of animal lovers. All the same, much may depend on the question whether our duties towards animals are direct or indirect, as we shall see in later chapters.

If one claims – surely rightly – that works of art lack moral standing, then it is obvious that this should not be taken as an attack upon art lovers. It is perfectly consistent with such a claim that one should care deeply about some, if not all, works of art, and that one should strive as hard as one can in the cause of their preservation. In the same way, the claim that animals lack moral standing should not be regarded as an attack upon animal lovers. It is entirely consistent with it that one should continue to admire, be amused by, or be besotted with animals – even that one should prefer the company of one's cat or dog to the company of human beings.

The general point is that not all values are moral ones. Many of us have projects or interests that occupy our attention and enrich our existence without making any moral claims upon us. One test for whether a value is a moral one is whether ignoring it should invite blame. While I might be sorry if I were somehow to lose my love of classical music, I do not think that it would be wrong of me if I were, in consequence, to cease going to concerts. In contrast, even if I were somehow to lose my respect for other people's property, it would still be blameworthy of me to steal. Another test is whether one should be prepared to generalise the claim in question to others. While I love to go walking in the wilderness, I recognise that this is not an interest that everyone shares, nor am I prepared to insist that they *should* share it. In contrast, if I value human liberty, to the extent of finding slavery abhorrent whatever the circumstances, I shall blame those who continue to traffic in human lives or who are otherwise indifferent to the value of freedom.

Our main question, to repeat, is whether animals have moral standing. But it should be remembered that a negative reply need not entail that there are no moral constraints on our treatment of animals.

THEORY AND PRACTICE

The overall topic of this book is directly practical – how should we behave towards animals, and why? Yet although this question is indeed a practical one, it should be obvious that in answering it we shall need to engage in theoretical discussion, concerning the nature and source of moral judgements. If we are to discover how far moral considerations may reach (that is, the boundaries of those who have moral standing), we shall need to investigate the basis of morality itself.

One theoretical issue arises immediately, since it threatens to render all further discussion pointless. This is the question whether moral judgements are merely subjective expressions of attitude. On such an account, some people just happen to have the attitude that animal suffering should be avoided, whereas some just happen to be indifferent. In which case, further discussion and argument are a waste of time. For example, if making the statement 'Hurting animals is wrong' is a bit like saying 'I dislike cheese', then there is really nothing more to be said. Or rather, if more is to be said it should be in the mode of mere rhetoric, rather than of rational argument. For it would obviously be foolish to try to *argue* someone out of their attitude to cheese. In the same way, it might be suggested, it would be foolish to try to argue someone out of their attitude towards animals. If such attitudes are to be changed, it will be by means other than rational persuasion.[1] In which case, if the business of philosophy is rational argument, as I believe it is, then on such matters philosophers should remain silent.

This strong subjectivist thesis is plainly false, however. It is a matter of common experience that moral beliefs are amenable to argument, in a way that questions of taste are not. For example, people generally feel constrained to try to resolve contradictions amongst their moral beliefs, attempting to find general principles that will reconcile them; whereas they feel no such constraint in connection with matters of taste. Thus, someone who believes on the one hand that abortion is always wrong (even to save the life of the mother), and who believes on the other hand that the blanket-bombing of German cities in the Second World War was justified, can easily be made to feel uncomfortable. For these both appear to be examples of the killing of innocents in pursuit of some further purpose. Note, however, that I do not claim that the beliefs in question *are* contradictory. There are a number of possible ways in which they might be reconciled. My point is only that people generally feel rationally constrained to attempt such a reconciliation. In contrast, no one will feel uneasy at disliking cheese but liking yoghurt, even when it is pointed out to them that both are dairy products.

While moral judgements are clearly amenable to reason, to a degree, this is not yet to say that they are objective. For we can distinguish between strong and weak versions of subjectivism. Strong subjectivism is the thesis we have just been considering, which holds that moral judgements are direct expressions of attitude or feeling. Weak subjectivism, on the other hand, would only claim that moral judgements depend ultimately upon the basic attitudes of the person making the judgement. While this may allow room for reason and argument within morality, it still remains possible for moral disagreements to be irreconcilable. In the end, different people may be committed to different basic principles, between which reason cannot adjudicate. Both of these varieties of subjectivism may be contrasted with an objectivist account of morality, which would maintain that in any moral dispute one or other of the disputants must be wrong, and that it must be possible, in principle at least, to establish who (if either) is right.

For our purposes it may not matter very much whether

morality is objective or weakly subjective. Each of these theories allows space for reason and argument within the moral sphere, and both can motivate a search for basic principles. Indeed, each of the two main moral theories to be considered in detail in the next chapter (namely, utilitarianism and contractualism) can be regarded in either of these lights. I do in fact believe, however, that most of those philosophers who have supported the weak subjectivist line have only done so because they have failed to distinguish between two different strengths of *objectivism*. Thinking, rightly, that strong objectivism is to be rejected, they have believed themselves thereby committed to some version of subjectivism. But this is a mistake. There remains the possibility of a weak objectivist interpretation of morality, as we shall see shortly.

Another point is this. In practice it will be hard to tell whether or not we have reached a disagreement that is truly fundamental, in the weak subjectivist sense. Even though the existence of irreconcilable moral viewpoints may be a theoretical possibility, in practice a weak subjectivist should allow that we may never be able to tell whether or not further debate might make a difference. Our moral judgements and principles are sufficiently complex that they (like beliefs in philosophy) are subject to constant revisability. Although someone may think that they have articulated their fundamental moral principle, from commitment to which nothing could rationally move them, in fact it can never be ruled out that there may yet be some comparison, analogy, or argument that would force them to reconsider.

On any defensible account of morality, then, general theoretical considerations may have a large part to play in determining our practical judgements. In morality, as in many other areas of our cognition (excepting matters of taste), we feel obliged, when we reflect on the matter, to try to make overall sense of our beliefs and attitudes. We should perhaps agree, indeed, that our moral beliefs can only really be acceptable if they form part of a coherent body of such beliefs, linked together by general principles having at least a powerful intuitive appeal. It follows that a considerable part of our task, when it comes to determining the appropriate moral treatment of animals, will consist in seeing how principles concerning such treatment might fit acceptably in to an overall moral theory.

MORAL THEORY, COMMON-SENSE BELIEF, AND ANIMALS

What relationship should obtain between our common-sense moral beliefs and our best moral theory? Will common sense only be vindicated if it can be grounded in an independently plausible theory? Or, on the contrary, can we take common sense for granted, so that any acceptable theory is constrained to account for it? The answer, in my view, is 'neither' (or, alternatively, 'partly both'). The proper relationship between common-sense moral belief and moral theory is best understood in terms of the concept of *reflective equilibrium*. This was first expounded by John Rawls in connection with a version of theory often known as contractualism,[2] but it is in fact equally applicable to other theoretical approaches.

The idea is that we should seek a position of equilibrium between theory and ordinary judgement that we can, on reflection, find rationally acceptable. We begin with our considered common-sense moral beliefs, having done our best to purge those beliefs of confusion, inconsistency, partiality, and prejudice. We then try to construct a plausible theory that will explain and give unity to those judgements. It may emerge, however, that the theory as proposed entails that some of those judgements are false. At this point we can either return to the theory and tinker with it until it delivers the right results, or we can give up an element of common-sense belief. Which option will be more reasonable will depend upon details. For example, if the theory is an attractive one and our best attempts to improve on it only produce modifications that appear to be entirely arbitrary, then we may opt to reject common sense. This will be especially plausible if we can provide some independent explanation of how ordinary people can have come to be deluded on the issue. Alternatively, if the belief in question is very firmly held, then our only reasonable course may be to give up or modify our theory. The overall goal is to reach a position that we can, on balance, be satisfied with.

On this view, the business of constructing an acceptable moral theory must take its start from common sense, in that our considered pre-theoretical judgements provide the data to be either accounted for or explained away, yet a particular moral belief, in its turn, will only be justified if it can be integrated into an acceptable moral theory. As we shall see later, there are a number of powerful constraints on the acceptability of moral theories, besides internal consistency. So it must be left open as a possibility at the out-set that a good deal of common-sense morality might have to be rejected, in the end, as a result of our theoretical reflections.

What shows, however, that the process of seeking reflective equilibrium is a necessary one to go through? Why should it be supposed that this is the only way to justify a set of moral beliefs? The answer is that (in contrast with mathematics, for example) there is no such thing as *proof* in ethics. For in the moral domain there are no fixed points, no beliefs about which we may be completely certain, that we could use as a foundation on which to erect a system of moral knowledge. There are no theoretical principles or common-sense beliefs that can be known for certain to be true in advance of investigating their relationships with our best considered theories and beliefs. So any moral theory must be tested, in part, by its consequences for common-sense belief, and the justification for a common-sense belief, in turn, will partly depend upon its capacity to receive a theoretical explanation. The justification-relation is mutual and reciprocal.

A comparison with our mode of knowledge of the physical world may be helpful at this point. Since René Descartes's *Meditations on First Philosophy* were published in 1641, the theory of knowledge has been dominated, until recently, by the idea generally known as *foundationalism*. On this view, some of our knowledge (generally held to be reports of immediate experience, or sense data, together with simple truths of reason) must be completely certain, to provide the foundation on which all other knowledge is to be erected. But this conception has

come under increasing pressure in recent decades, and rightly so
– in part because of doubts about whether there really is
anything that can be known for certain. Many philosophers
have, in consequence, come to endorse an opposing *coherentism*
about our knowledge. They have come to see the justification
for our beliefs about the world in terms of overall explanatory
coherence, in which the relations of support between our
various beliefs are mutual and reciprocal.[3] The concept of
reflective equilibrium is best seen as an application of the
coherentist picture of knowledge to the moral domain. And it is,
if anything, even more unavoidable here, since in this domain
there are simply no candidates for beliefs that might serve as a
foundation, carrying their justification in and of themselves.

Since our task is to investigate the relationship between moral
theory and the question of the moral standing of animals,
seeking a position of reflective equilibrium on the issue, it will be
useful to have a rough idea at the out-set of what our common-
sense morality tells us about the status and appropriate
treatment of animals. The general view seems to imply that
animals have *partial* moral standing – their lives and experiences
having direct moral significance, but much less than that of
human beings. Most people hold that it is wrong to cause
animals unnecessary suffering. Opinions will differ as to what
counts as necessary. Some would say that the suffering caused
by the testing of detergents is permissible. Others would allow
suffering only in the course of genuine scientific experiments.
Yet others would allow animals to suffer only in the course of
important medical experiments. But all will agree that gra-
tuitous suffering – suffering caused for no good reason – is
wrong. To cause such suffering is generally recognised to be
cruel. (I think all would also agree that the sufferings of animals
cannot be weighed against the sufferings of human beings,
though I shall defer developing this point to the final sections of
Chapter 3.)

When it comes to killing, I think common-sense morality tells
us that the killing of animals is not wrong, except for no good
reason. Again, opinions will differ as to what counts as good
reason. Some would allow that animals may be killed for sport

(perhaps provided that the manner of the killing is not cruel). Others would allow them to be killed for the pleasure of eating their flesh. Yet others would allow them to be killed only to protect legitimate human interests, as when rabbits are shot to prevent crop damage. And others again will only allow animals to be killed where human lives are at stake, as when meat is the only available food. But all will agree that there is no question of weighing up animal lives against the lives of humans.

To see this last point, imagine that you arrive at a fire in a dogs' home to find Kenneth, the human owner, unconscious on the floor while the dogs are all locked in their cages. Your judgement is that you only have time to drag Kenneth to safety, or to unlock the cages to allow the dogs to escape, but not both. Here I think no one would maintain that you ought to place the lives of many dogs above the life of a single human. Whereas most would believe that, in an otherwise comparable situation in which only humans were involved, the best thing to do would be to save as many lives as possible. This is always supposing, of course, that all else is equal. If Kenneth is known to be a mass murderer or child molester then many might feel differently about the case. The common-sense view seems to be that human beings can, by their own actions, forfeit their right to life, or cease to be worth rescuing.

It is worth stressing, since it will prove to be of some importance later, that our common-sense belief that human and animal lives cannot be weighed against one another appears to be particularly central to morality, or especially firmly held. For even those philosophers who have been most vociferous in promoting the rights of animals, such as Tom Regan and Peter Singer, go to considerable lengths to retain it.[4] If we are to be forced to give up this aspect of common-sense morality, it will require, at the least, a theoretical argument that is very powerful indeed.

AN EXAMPLE, AND SOME REACTIONS

I shall now present and discuss a particular example, not directly related to the animals issue. It will serve, both to introduce a variety of theoretical approaches to morality, and also as a test of the reader's own beliefs and attitudes. The example is based upon a real case (as are many of the examples to be used in this book). I have changed some of the details, however, as well as the names of the people involved.

Some years ago a married couple committed joint suicide. Anthony was a famous author in his seventies, facing a painful terminal illness that would involve gradual loss of the mental faculties he valued so highly. His wife Susie, however, was in her forties and healthy. The couple had no children. They discussed their situation extensively before reaching a decision. Both were agreed that an early death would provide a merciful release for Anthony, and after careful consideration Susie decided that she did not wish to go on living without him. It should be plain to us that she made a disastrous mistake, nevertheless. Grief, no matter how debilitating, is not terminal. It is a cliché, but true, that time heals all. We can be confident that had Anthony alone committed suicide Susie would have been able to pick up the threads of her life again, though perhaps after an extensive period of mourning, and that she would probably have gone on to lead a fruitful and satisfying existence. Two questions then arise about Susie's decision. First, was her suicide not just mistaken, but morally wrong or blameworthy? Second, supposing that we had known of the situation in advance, would we have been under a moral obligation to try to prevent her? Let us now canvass some of the possible avenues of response.

Some people will be inclined to say that Susie's suicide was definitely wrong because it involved the termination of a human life, and human life is sacred. In the same vein, they will say that had we known in advance of her decision we would have been obliged to act to prevent her death, so as to preserve something sacred. Such people have an approach to ethics that is at bottom theistic, believing, in one version, that moral goodness is to be identified with what God approves of, and that moral duties are to be identified with God's commands. (Other versions may hold that it is essential to our notion of moral goodness that such goodness is exemplified in the person of God, and that our duties are revealed to us by example, as in the life of Jesus Christ. These differences of detail need not concern us.) The theistic theory of morality will be discussed in the section that follows.

Others may agree that what Susie did was wrong, and that we ought to have intervened had we known what she was going to do, but hold these beliefs on somewhat different grounds. They may claim that human life is (at least normally) intrinsically valuable. So Susie's suicide involved the destruction of something having intrinsic value, just as a murder would have done, quite apart from the question whether there is a God who disapproves of what she did. Such people maintain that it is a given fact about the world that some things, including human lives, are valuable in their own right, giving rise to obligations on our part to respect and preserve those values wherever possible. (Some versions of belief in the sacredness of human life really come down to this, if it is held that the reason why God disapproves of suicide or murder is *because* human life is intrinsically valuable.) This theory, too, will shortly receive a section to itself.

Another way of responding to the example would be to maintain that we should look at the likely consequences of Susie's act, for good or harm. This theory (or family of theories) goes under the name of utilitarianism. In its simplest version it holds that an action is right if and only if it causes a greater balance of happiness over unhappiness than would any alternative action. A utilitarian will almost certainly maintain that Susie acted wrongly. For her untimely death cut off a generally worthwhile future existence for herself, and also prevented her from contributing to the happiness of others, as she probably would have done had she lived. A utilitarian will also be likely to hold that we would have been obliged to prevent Susie's suicide if we could, since this would have secured more happiness overall. But this judgement will depend, additionally, upon the likely costs to us of our intervention, as well as on the possible detrimental effects on Susie's happiness of having had the decision taken out of her own hands. Utilitarianism comes in many shapes and guises, and has been defended in one version or another by many distinguished thinkers. It will receive extensive discussion in Chapter 2.

A final way of responding to Susie's suicide would be to maintain that her action cannot have been wrong, since it violated no one's rights. She was in fact under no contract or obligation to continue her life (as, perhaps, she would have been had she had children in need of her care). On the contrary, she was a free agent, having the right to act in matters affecting only herself as she saw fit. Someone taking this line will probably also hold that we would have had no right to intervene to prevent Susie's death, provided we were aware that her decision was taken after due consideration, by one who was of sound mind and under no duress. While we would have been morally permitted, perhaps obliged, to try to persuade her to reconsider, ultimately it was her own business. Morality is here viewed as a set of rules to govern interactions between agents, placing constraints on what they may legitimately do to one another, but otherwise leaving them free to pursue their own plans and projects. This theory, too, comes in many different versions, and has been defended by a variety of distinguished thinkers. In its most popular forms it may be known as contractualism, since moral rules are pictured as resulting from a certain kind of imaginary contract, as we shall see later. Contractualism, too, will receive extensive discussion in Chapter 2.

I have outlined a variety of ethical theories, all of which can find a foothold, at least, in the reflections of ordinary people. It is now time to turn to the business of assessment. Part of our task will be to lay down some general constraints that any adequate theory of morality should meet, quite aside from its ability to explain our considered common-sense beliefs.

THEISTIC ETHICS

As we saw above, some thinkers claim that moral goodness is to be identified with what God approves of, and that moral duties are to be identified with God's commands. Believing that God has forbidden us to kill, either ourselves or one another, they will then maintain that Susie, the suicide, acts wrongly. When considering the question of the moral standing of animals, such theorists may perhaps adduce evidence that God disapproves of people who cause suffering to animals, but less than he disapproves of those who cause suffering to human beings. So this theory at least stands some chance of being successful in accommodating common-sense beliefs about the moral standing of animals.

Whatever one's religious beliefs, this view should be rejected, for reasons I shall explain in a moment. But an initial strategic difficulty for the theist is that arguments from such a standpoint are unlikely to carry conviction in our increasingly secular age. It is no good trying to convince someone that something is morally wrong on the grounds that God has forbidden it, unless you are also prepared to try to convince them that God exists. But in fact the reasons for this latter belief are highly controversial.[5] So theists, nowadays, are certainly well advised to look for secular arguments in support of their moral beliefs.

In fact the thesis that moral goodness reduces to what God approves of (or exemplifies) was decisively refuted by Plato in his dialogue *Euthyphro* (*c.* 380 BC), many years before the birth of Christ. Plato sets this thesis a dilemma, asking whether what is good is approved of by God *because it is good*, or whether it is good *because God approves of it*. On the first alternative, God's approval is mere evidence of moral goodness, and some independent account must be possible of what makes that thing good. If we take the second alternative, on the other hand, then we must be supposed to have no conception of moral goodness independent of God's approval. In which case, if God had approved of the regular torture and sacrifice of little children, then that would have been morally good. But this conclusion is outrageous. It might be replied that God could not have approved of the torture of children, because God is good. But this is to concede the point. For it implies that we do, after all, have some conception of moral goodness that is independent of God's approval. Otherwise we could not know that a wholly good God could not approve of such things.

Either way, then, it follows that morality has a subject-matter that is independent of the question of God's approval or commands. In which case, our considered moral views, arrived at on the best available secular grounds, should constrain our interpretations of the Bible and other religious texts, in the same way that our considered astronomical and geological views should constrain our interpretations of those texts. Since these texts are, at best, the word of God filtered through the minds of human beings, we should dismiss or reinterpret what is inconsistent with our considered non-theological beliefs. For example, if our best secular view is that there is no moral objection to homosexuality, then St Paul's condemnation of homosexuality should be dismissed as Paul the man of his time speaking, rather than accepted as the word of God. On the animals issue, therefore, the primary question to be answered is whether or not our best secular theories of morality would accord moral standing to animals.

STRONG OBJECTIVITY AND INTUITIONISM

As we saw earlier, in connection with the example of Susie, the suicide, many people will be tempted by the idea that some things (including human lives) possess intrinsic value, making claims on us that are objective and inescapable. Such views have been gaining increasing currency recently. This is especially so amongst members of the ecology movement, some of whom have seized on the idea of intrinsic value as providing a basis on which to argue that we have direct duties towards the environment. Since, they claim, rain forests and rare species of animal possess intrinsic value, we are morally obliged not to collude in their destruction. As we shall see, however, it is ill-advised to try to vindicate the ecology movement in this manner, since the theory of intrinsic value turns out to be indefensible.

In its purest forms this sort of theory is known as intuitionism. A version of it was defended by G. E. Moore in his book *Principia Ethica*,[6] though it has had many other adherents. The intuitionist maintains that moral values really exist, independently of us, and that we may know of them through acts of intellectual intuition – a kind of 'seeing with the mind's eye'. I shall do my best to explain this doctrine, setting it within a more general contrast between strong and weak objectivism. But I shall then go on to argue that intuitionism provides an unacceptable framework for moral theory. In the final section of the chapter I shall show that one famous defence of animal rights might best be classed as a kind of intuitionism, and, if it is, that it should be rejected for that reason.

Just as we earlier distinguished between strong and weak versions of subjectivism, so too we can distinguish between strong and weak versions of objectivism. Strong objectivism claims that morality deals with values that are *given*, that somehow form part of the fabric of the world. Weak objectivism, on the other hand, claims only that ethics employs concepts (ideas in our minds) with determinate conditions of application. In order to see clearly the nature of the contrast being drawn here, let us look at how the same distinction will apply to the difference between science, on the one hand, and common-sense beliefs about the physical world, on the other.

One distinctive feature of scientific discourse is that in science we try to match our concepts to *real divisions in nature*. Thus we believe, for example, that early scientists were mistaken in classifying whales and porpoises as fish. Although whales, like sharks, live in the sea, it turns out that they have little in common with other sea creatures when it comes to explaining their behaviour, their evolution, and their natural life-cycle. In contrast with science, in ordinary life we often employ concepts for other (non-explanatory) purposes that can yield objective truths without having to correspond to real divisions in nature. We employ concepts like 'table' and 'spice', for example, that collect together things that are, from a scientific point of view, really quite heterogeneous. But for all that, it is objectively true that I am sitting at a table as I write this, and that I ate spiced food last night.

In terms of the distinctions explained earlier, science is strongly objective whereas many common-sense beliefs about the physical world are only weakly objective. Both consist of statements with determinate conditions of application. In both cases, whether or not a statement is true is independent of the beliefs and attitudes of those who make the statement – both assume that truth is to be discovered, not invented. But common sense employs concepts that carve up the world to suit our purposes, in ways that may cut against the joints. While it is true that I am sitting at a table, and hence true that individual tables really exist, the difference between tables and other types of thing is not itself a part of the real world. It is rather something we impose on the world, in selecting the concepts we do. In science, on the other hand, the statement that sharks are fish is true only if the distinction we draw between fish and other types of thing corresponds to a real difference – that is, a difference that is already there in the world, helping to govern its operation and causal processes.

Moral intuitionists believe that morality, like science, is strongly objective. Of course they do not think that moral concepts are scientific ones, or that moral properties will figure in causal explanations. But they think that moral facts and moral distinctions are somehow given, being already there in the world, placing a constraint upon any acceptable ethic. On this view, there is a real difference between those things that have value and those things that do not, which is entirely independent of us and our system of concepts (ideas). On the contrary, if we were to attempt to classify the value of things in any other manner than the way in which they are really distinguished, then we should be making a mistake, and all statements involving those concepts would be false.

Scientists hope that we may come to know the real divisions in nature by observation and experiment, and by reasoning to the best explanation of the phenomena we observe. Plainly, however, our mode of knowledge of morality must be different.

We cannot literally see the moral value of a thing, or know it by inference to the best explanation of what we see. Moral intuitionists maintain that we nevertheless have access to the real divisions of value in the world, by means of a special faculty of intellectual intuition. We may know whether or not something is really valuable by imagining it existing entirely on its own, and asking ourselves whether it is a good thing that it should exist. Intuitionists believe that the answers that intuitively come to us in such circumstances are generally reliable, providing us with knowledge of moral properties that is strongly objective.

Intuitionists may then hope to provide an easy vindication of our common-sense attitude towards animals. They may say that when we imagine, entirely on its own, an animal in pain, we can see intuitively that this is an intrinsically bad state of affairs; but that when we imagine a situation in which the suffering of an animal is necessary to prevent some degree of dissatisfaction or injury to a human being, then we can see intuitively that it is no longer wrong. Similarly, they may say that when we imagine the death of an animal we can see that this is the loss of something intrinsically valuable; but that when we imagine the same death being necessary to prevent some human suffering, or to preserve some human life, then we can see that the situation is no longer a bad one. It follows, intuitionists may claim, that while animal experience and life is of some value, it is less valuable than the experiences and lives of human beings[7] – which is just what common sense tells us.

AGAINST INTUITIONISM

While moral intuitionism might have provided a vindication of our common-sense attitudes towards animals, it seems to me to be plainly unacceptable. One argument for this conclusion is what Mackie calls 'the argument from queerness'.[8] If moral values really exist in the objective world, then they must be very peculiar entities indeed. They are not actually present in physical objects, in the way that properties like mass and shape are. Nor, presumably, do they have any causal role. Unlike the sorts of properties in the natural world recognised by science, moral values do not serve to explain, in causal terms, the behaviour of physical objects and systems. They are rather, as Moore put it, *non-natural* properties. The very queerness of the idea of properties that have real existence, but that exist outside of the natural order, is an argument against accepting it.

This queerness can be emphasised still further by noting that moral properties must somehow be such as to *supervene upon* natural ones. For everyone agrees that there can be no differences in the values of things without some corresponding difference in their natural properties. There surely could not be two actions or agents exactly alike in all natural respects – for example, two acts done with the same intention and causing precisely the same degree of damage or pain – but differing in moral value. But if moral properties were genuinely objective, and existed outside of the natural order, then this supervenience would be extremely puzzling, to say the least. For if moral properties lie *outside* the natural world, then how does it come that they cannot apply to things independently of facts *within* the natural world?

Even more of a problem is presented by the task of explaining the operation (or, indeed, the very existence) of our supposed faculty of intuition. Given that moral values do not form part of the natural world, then how are they supposed to have an effect upon our minds? How can something that is not in nature have an effect upon something that is? Indeed, it seems peculiar to think of moral values as being causes at all. How is the property of being valuable supposed to give rise to beliefs in us about it? How, for example, would the objective fact that humans are more valuable than dogs be supposed to cause in our minds the intuition that they are more valuable? The very idea seems barely intelligible.

Even supposing that the hypothesis made sense, that an objective value might be able to cause beliefs in our minds, it would still remain inexplicable, in natural terms, how we could have come to possess a faculty of mind that would allow us to gain knowledge in such a manner. For in order to have been selected in evolution, a faculty of moral intuition would have to have conferred survival value on those first humans who happened to possess it, or a primitive version of it. But it seems unlikely that a faculty of moral intuition could have conferred any survival value. In contrast, the faculty of sight is easily explained, since there are all sorts of ways in which you will be better able to survive if you can see things accurately.

It might be replied that moral beliefs have obvious survival value, since human beings who lacked them would not be able to function effectively together in co-operative societies. But this is not to the point. The problem is to explain how we could come to have a faculty of mind giving us *reliable* access to features of an objective moral realm, not to explain why we should have moral beliefs at all. From the point of view of evolution, it would not matter in the least if all of our moral beliefs about the moral realm were false, provided that they were nevertheless such as to enable us to co-operate together in society.

Even supposing that the idea of a faculty for intuiting moral values made sense, and that we could somehow explain the fact that we possess it, there would remain good reasons for doubting its reliability. For it is obvious that people's moral intuitions not only can, but do, conflict. Indeed, their intuitions seem, to a remarkable degree, to reflect the norms that are current in their surrounding society. (This is another reason why common-sense moral beliefs need the backing of moral theory, if they are to be rationally acceptable. Otherwise there can be no adjudicating between conflicting intuitions.) A country-dweller may intuit that there is nothing wrong with drowning a kitten, whereas to a town-dweller it may seem intuitively that this is inexcusable. Someone in a slave-owning society may claim to see intuitively that the lives of slaves are less valuable than the lives of free men, whereas we will intuit the opposite. Someone in a patriarchal society may intuit that the life of a woman is less valuable than that of her male child. And so it goes. If we really did possess a faculty of moral intuition, then its operation would seem to be determined, not so much by whatever objective values there may or may not be, but by the moral beliefs that are already current within our society.

What follows is that intuitionism seems inevitably to lead to moral scepticism. Since we have good reason to doubt the reliability of our faculty of moral intuition (supposing that we possess such a thing), we have reason to doubt our individual moral judgements. There would seem to be no particular reason, indeed, to think that our faculty of intuition is *ever* accurate. For those moral beliefs that are universal, such as injunctions against arbitrary killings, may be explained in terms of the requirements that are necessary for a human society to function and flourish, rather than as the result of the reliable operation of our faculty of intuition. If intuitionism is a correct moral theory, then for all we know *all* of our beliefs about moral value may be wrong. I take it that this conclusion is too extreme to be acceptable.

For all of the above reasons, intuitionism is simply un-believable as a theory of morality. If we are inclined to think that moral judgements are objective, then it would be far more acceptable to endorse some version of weak objectivism. We could maintain that we have developed moral concepts to suit our purposes, just as we have evolved concepts like 'chair' and 'spice'. Given those concepts, it can be objectively true that certain actions are right, or wrong, despite the fact that the difference between right and wrong does not itself exist in the world, any more than the difference between spices and other foodstuffs itself exists in the world. On such an account, indeed, knowledge that someone has done something wrong can be just as much a matter of (ordinary, sensory) perception as is the knowledge that they are seated on a chair. To perceive a chair is to perceive an item in the physical world *as* an instance of the concept 'chair'. Then so, too, for a weak objectivist, in the case of perception of moral facts – to perceive that someone is doing something wrong is to perceive an event in the physical world *as* an instance of the concept 'wrong'. All of this is entirely unmysterious by comparison with intuitionism, although, of course, the main business of giving an account of the substantial content of moral concepts remains. What follows in Chapter 2 can be seen as a contribution to that task.

REGAN ON RIGHTS

One of the main philosophical champions of animal rights has been Tom Regan.[9] His writings contain many useful insights and challenging arguments, some of which will be considered in later chapters. But I shall argue here that his position is either, at bottom, a form of sophisticated intuitionism (and may thus be dismissed as such), or it fails to provide us with something that we have a right to demand of any moral theory, if it is to be acceptable – namely, a *governing conception* (as I shall call it) of the origins of morality and moral motivation. All this will take some explaining.

Regan is explicit in employing the method of reflective equilibrium. He sees the business of moral theory to be the discovery of moral principles that can regularise and explain our considered moral judgements. (These are the judgements, remember, that we would make when we try as hard as we can to attain moral truth, but before introducing considerations of theory.) He argues that the most acceptable principles that we can find are, in fact, ones that ascribe certain basic rights, not only to all human beings, but to animals as well. His position is thus partly a defence of common sense, in that animals get accorded moral standing. But it is also a revision of common sense, in that the rights assigned to animals go well beyond what most ordinary people would allow.

At the heart of Regan's position is the thesis that all creatures who are 'subjects-of-a-life' (that is, who have beliefs and desires, and at least a rudimentary sense of their own past and future – Regan takes this to include all mammals aged one or more) possess equal intrinsic moral value.[10] This value is not to be analysed in terms of possession of moral rights, but rather forms the ground of the claim that all subjects-of-a-life possess an equal right to respect. (Such an equality of intrinsic value has to be postulated, Regan thinks, if we are to account for our belief that all human beings possess the same basic moral rights, irrespective of differences of intelligence and moral character. This argument will be challenged, and replied to, in Chapter 5.) Now, one natural reading of the thesis that creatures of a certain kind possess equal moral value *intrinsically* is that it involves a commitment to strong objectivism. The idea would be that all subjects-of-a-life have a value that inheres in them independently of our knowledge or existence. This would make Regan a kind of sophisticated intuitionist.

Admittedly, Regan does not use the language of 'intuition' or 'seeing with the mind's eye'. But it is hard to see how the method of reflective equilibrium could gain us access to the objective values that are supposed to exist in the world, unless we did possess some special faculty of intellectual intuition to underpin it. That Regan ducks out of grounding his moral theory in any developed theory of our knowledge of moral facts does not mean that we are not owed some such account. And it is hard to see how any story he could tell here would not be at least as implausible as the intuitionist one we rejected in the last section.

It may be, on the other hand, that Regan's theory can be regarded much more neutrally. If we take seriously the way in which he presents the method of reflective equilibrium, then we could see him as only intending to find moral principles that can explain and unify a maximal proportion of our considered common-sense beliefs. Read in this way, the claim that all subjects-of-a-life possess equal intrinsic value may only amount to the claim that it would be most reasonable for us to adopt the principle of *valuing* all subjects-of-a-life equally, irrespective of their other attributes and the differences between them. There is nothing in this to commit Regan to strong objectivism, or any form of intuitionism.

I have no quarrel with the method of reflective equilibrium as such. As a method, indeed, it will loom large in the chapters that follow. But I do want to insist that it cannot be the whole story. Or, perhaps better, I want to insist that when properly understood, reflective equilibrium involves a good deal more than merely finding principles to explain and unify considered common-sense belief. A good moral theory must also give us a plausible picture of the sources of morality and moral knowledge, and of the source of moral motivation. Thus our rejection of intuitionism, above, is best understood as an application of

the method of reflective equilibrium. The reason why intuitionism is unacceptable as a theory is because it cannot provide
a plausible account of the subject-matter of morality, of our
knowledge of it, or, indeed, of why we should care about the
values that are supposed to exist independently of us.

Once strong subjectivism and theistic theories of ethics have
been rejected, it becomes pressing to know how there can be
such a thing as morality at all. We need an explanation of how
moral notions can arise, that will at the same time explain how
these notions can make demands on us that are, in some sense,
rational. For it is plain that morality is not just another special
interest, like stamp-collecting, which people may or may not
have. Another way to put the point is that in morality we have
a putative body of knowledge – people claim to *know* that child-
abuse is wrong, for example – and a theory of morality needs to
provide some account of what this knowledge is knowledge *of*. It
also needs to explain why it is that we care so deeply about
morality, thus characterised – we need to be told what is it
about morality that enables it to claim such a central place in
our lives.

Regan's attempt to ground a theory of rights, and to show
that animals have rights, falls short in just these respects. For he
gives no account of where rights are supposed to have come
from, nor of why we should care about them once they have
arrived. (Indeed, as we shall see in later chapters, many of his
specific arguments for his views, and against the views of others,
simply cannot be successful in the absence of such an account.)
We can draw a general moral from his failure. It is this: if a
theory of morality is to stand any chance of being acceptable, it
should consist of two rather different, though related, aspects.
First, an ethical theory should contain a *governing conception* of the
nature of morality. This will provide a distinctive picture of the
source of moral notions and moral knowledge, and of the basis
of moral motivation. Second, and distinct from, though perhaps
derived from the first, an ethical theory should contain some
basic normative principle or principles that are to guide our
judgements of right and wrong.

We can say, then, that there are two main requirements that

a moral theory must meet, if it is to be rationally acceptable. The first is that its governing conception must give us a plausible picture of the source of morality, and of the origins of moral motivation. This is where Regan fails altogether. The second is less deeply theoretical, but equally important. It is that the basic normative principle or principles of the theory should yield intuitively acceptable consequences. But it is important to stress that this is not a retreat towards intuitionism. There need be no commitment to special mental faculties for obtaining moral knowledge, or to the real existence of values in the world. It is simply that a good moral theory must entail at least a fair proportion of our considered moral beliefs, at the cost, otherwise, of becoming unbelievable. Any moral theory that could justify arbitrary killings of innocents, for example, is going to be unacceptable, no matter how satisfying it may seem in respect of its governing conception. The next chapter will be occupied with exploring the relative strengths and weaknesses of utilitarianism and contractualism along each of these two dimensions.

SUMMARY

I have argued that both strong subjectivism and strong objectivism are unacceptable as accounts of morality – moral judgements are neither direct expressions of attitude or feeling, nor descriptive of values that exist independent of the human mind and human systems of classification. But both weak subjectivism and weak objectivism are left in play – it may be that moral disagreements express, at bottom, commitment to different basic principles, or it may be that they result from the complexities inherent in a common system of concepts. But either way, fully justifying a moral belief must involve showing how it may be integrated into a moral theory whose governing conception and basic normative principles are each acceptable after rational reflection.

CHAPTER 2

Utilitarianism and contractualism

In this chapter I shall examine two theories (or classes of theory) that stand some chance of proving acceptable, both in respect of the explanations provided by their governing conceptions of the source of moral notions and moral motivation, and in respect of their basic normative output. The theories are utilitarianism and contractualism.

UTILITARIANISM AND ITS GOVERNING CONCEPTION

Although utilitarianism is named after its basic normative principle (the principle of utility), and although not all utilitarian thinkers have felt the need to provide their theory with a governing conception, I shall begin my discussion by outlining what I take that conception to be. The main idea is that morality may be viewed as the set of decisions that would be made by an impartial benevolent observer – an observer who is aware of all the conflicting interests in a given situation, and of the consequences that different policies would have for those interests, and who is equally sympathetic towards all of the parties involved. The governing conception of utilitarianism is thus an imaginary construction (as is the governing conception of contractualism, as we shall see later). The moral point of view is a sort of God's eye view, but independent of any belief in an actual God. It is the point of view that we would take if we could be fully aware of all the consequences of our actions, and could be equally sympathetic towards all those affected.

Plausibly, what an impartial benevolent observer would always choose is the option that would have as a consequence the greatest happiness, or desire satisfaction, or pleasure. (These formulations are not exactly equivalent and lead to rather different versions of utilitarianism. But the differences will not concern us, in general. Throughout most of this book I shall use 'utility' in a consciously ambiguous way, to equivocate between the different possible ultimate values of utilitarians, only being more precise when something of importance turns on the issue.) So the most basic normative principle of utilitarianism is that one should maximise overall utility (whether in total or on average – again there are differences here that need not concern us). For observers who are truly impartial will be indifferent as to whose utility is in question, and being truly benevolent, they will wish to do as much good as they can.

Most of the problems with utilitarianism arise from its basic normative principle, as we shall see shortly. In contrast, the greatest attraction of the theory lies in its governing conception. This can provide us with a satisfying explanation, not only of the origin of moral notions, but also of the source of moral motivation. Both explanations start from an hypothesis of natural (though limited) benevolence. This involves, like the contractualist accounts we shall consider later, a claim about an innately given aspect of human nature. The idea is that human beings will naturally feel an impulse of sympathy for the unhappiness, frustrated desires, or sufferings of other humans. Such an impulse will only actually occur, of course, when other things are equal – for example, in the absence of prior hatred for the individual in question. It will also only occur, in the first instance, in response to more or less direct confrontation with the suffering of another – as when one sees someone crying with grief over the dead body of a loved one, or observes them moaning from the pain of a broken leg. At any rate, it is surely very plausible that a normal person will feel sympathy in such a situation.

The next step in the explanation is that the natural impulse towards benevolence should become rationalised – developed and extended through the impact of rational considerations. For there is, plainly, no rational difference between the suffering of someone whom one can see, and the suffering of someone whom one does not. Nor is there any rational difference between the suffering of someone whom one knows and cares for, and the suffering of a stranger. Each of these types of suffering is equally real, and may be of equal severity. Reason then demands that one should respond equally. Hence the picture of the impartial observer – one should be equally sympathetic towards the sufferings of all those who suffer equally.

According to utilitarianism, then, morality arises in the first place when the natural impulse towards benevolence is universalised through the impact of reason. And then the source of moral motivation is that we cannot, by our very nature, avoid the sympathetic impulse; nor can we, in so far as we are rational, avoid its universalisation. These are very plausible explanations, avoiding the excesses of strong objectivism and intuitionism.

PROBLEMS WITH UTILITARIANISM

While the main strength of utilitarianism lies in its governing conception, its main weakness lies in its basic normative principle, the injunction to maximise utility. This gives rise to a number of notorious problems. The first is that it entails very counter-intuitive solutions to questions of distributive justice. Since all that utilitarianism regards as mattering, in the end, is total (or perhaps average) utility, the intense sufferings of a few can in principle be justified in terms of the marginal benefits of many. For example, one of the standard objections to utilitarianism is that it might be forced to legitimate a system of slavery, if the total number of slaves were few and the benefits to the slave-owners were sufficiently great. Yet, we would surely want to insist against this, that it is only the worst-off individuals who should be taken into account. (This intuition will be captured by the so-called *difference principle* of contractualism, as we shall see later.) Unless it can be shown that the slaves themselves must inevitably be even more degraded and unhappy under any realistic alternative to slavery, the system will stand morally condemned.

Consider a less dramatic example to make the same point. Suppose that Daniel is a doctor who possesses only a limited quantity of a very expensive drug. Unusually, this drug has a dual use – in very small quantities it can permanently cure acne, and in very large quantities it can cure some life-threatening disease. Daniel may, therefore, face a choice between removing a major source of unhappiness for many hundreds – perhaps thousands – of adolescents, and saving the life of a single individual. Here even the simplest of utilitarian calculations may show that the drug ought to be used as a cure for acne, allowing the individual in question to die. But this is hugely counter-intuitive. I think we should want to insist that the sufferings of the adolescents, although perfectly real, simply do not count when set against a person's life. (This does not imply that doctors ought never to prescribe aspirin for a headache, or to set a broken finger. In real life it is rare for them to be faced with choices as stark and clear as Daniel's.)

Utilitarians do have various avenues of reply to the problem of distributive justice. The most plausible of these is to appeal to some sort of two-tier system of morality, two rather different versions of which will be outlined shortly. But first let me introduce another traditional objection, which is that utilitarianism, in contrast with contractualism, cannot provide adequate protection for individuals. Apparently anything can be done to a person, provided that it produces more utility (either total or average) than any alternative course of action. One famous version of this objection is that a utilitarian may be forced to condone the judicial punishment of the innocent.

Consider the following example. Some years ago there was a series of murders of young black men in Atlanta, evidently performed by the same hand. The killings were thought to have a racial motive, and there were persistent rumours of police connivance in failing to catch the killer. These rumours sparked a series of race-riots, in which many people were killed and injured. Now suppose that Prunella, the state prosecutor, has come to believe that the killer was in fact white, but is now dead. Her evidence is not of such a nature to convince a court of law, however, or to bring an end to the riots. Now by some chance she stumbles across evidence that could easily be used to frame a particular black man. (She also has conclusive evidence, which she could easily suppress, that he was not in fact the killer.) What should Prunella do? As a utilitarian, it seems she should frame the man, resulting in one execution or life sentence, thus putting an end to the riots and saving many lives. But this seems intuitively abhorrent.

Notice that two of the considerations to which utilitarians often appeal, in trying to explain why judicial punishment of the innocent is wrong, have no application in this example. For since Prunella is the only one who will know that there has been a miscarriage of justice (aside from the person she frames, of course), there need be no long-term weakening of respect for the rule of law resulting from her action. Nor need the weakening of her own disposition towards the impartial application of the law have any bad consequences in the future. For we can imagine that she is on the point of retirement, and will henceforward have no role as an officer of the law.

Some utilitarians have tried to respond to these difficulties by retreating from the act-utilitarianism we have been considering so far, to a version of theory sometimes known as rule-utilitarianism. The idea is that, instead of actions being judged directly in terms of the utility of their consequences, actions should be judged by their conformity with a set of rules, and it is the rules that are justified by appeal to their general utility. These utilitarians have thus claimed that the rules outlawing slavery and forbidding the judicial punishment of the innocent are generally good ones, compliance with them producing the most utility in almost all cases. Then the actions of instituting a system of slavery, and of arranging for the punishment of an innocent man, are wrong because they conflict with rules justified by appeal to utility, even though in the particular case the actions in question may produce more utility than any alternative.

There can be no reflective equilibrium here, however. For rule-utilitarianism is an unstable position. There are two reasons for this. The first is that there is a problem about selecting the right rules (that is, the rules that accord with ordinary belief).

For in place of the rule forbidding judicial punishment of the innocent, why should we not adopt a rule that forbids such punishment *except* where the utility of doing so is very great and *except* where it can be known that there will be no weakening of respect for the law as a result? It certainly looks as though this rule would be productive of more utility in the long run, which lands us back with the original problem.

The second reason why the position is unstable is even more devastating. It is that rule-utilitarianism, as a basic normative principle, appears inconsistent with the governing conception of utilitarianism. For why would rationalised sympathy lead one, in the first instance, to justify a system of rules? It is the sufferings of individuals that matter, surely. Indeed, rule-utilitarianism appears vulnerable to the charge of unmotivated rule-worship.[1] For in a case where I can see clearly that breach of a rule would produce more utility than would compliance, what possible utilitarian justification can there be for insisting on compliance? If utilitarianism is to find a position of reflective equilibrium with ordinary belief, it needs to pursue a different strategy.

QUALITY-OF-CHARACTER-UTILITARIANISM

The way forward for utilitarians is to claim that the primary object of moral assessment is neither actions nor rules, but qualities of character. This is in fact the view of John Stuart Mill in *Utilitarianism* (1863), though Mill is often mistaken for a rule-utilitarian. It is also the view developed by Richard Hare in *Moral Thinking*.[2] The idea is that our primary duty is to develop qualities of character – dispositions of thought and feeling – whose possession is likely to produce the greatest overall utility. Such an account would be supposed to be grounded in a more realistic view of human rationality, and of the springs of human action, than is presupposed by act-utilitarianism.

It is often remarked that act-utilitarians seem to regard human beings as mere calculating machines. Their picture of moral agency requires that people should be constantly calculating the likely consequences of the various actions open to them on any given occasion. But this is unrealistic. Besides powers of rational calculation, we also have emotions and desires, and these are likely to exert a profound influence on our judgements of right and wrong. We also frequently find ourselves in situations where we are required to act quickly, without time for careful assessment of consequences, or estimates of resulting utility. The very least that can be said is that appropriate dispositions of thought and feeling are likely to make a very great difference to our effectiveness as utilitarian agents.

More importantly, since moral judgements are so susceptible to influence by emotion and desire, we may argue, on utilitarian grounds, that moral agents should develop dispositions of thought and feeling that exclude certain options from consideration. For example, it may be important that our law officers should never even think of breaking the rules, since they may otherwise be tempted into breaking the law in cases where they should not. Then, in the case of the Atlanta murders discussed earlier, a utilitarian may condemn Prunella for framing the man, because of the weakness in her moral character thereby displayed. This apparently accounts for our common-sense judgement, while allowing that the action did, in the circumstances, turn out for the best.

Compare, here, the utilitarian attitude to adultery. A utilitarian may be expected to argue that in principle some acts of adultery are permissible (because productive of more utility than would otherwise occur), but that in general adultery is wrong because of its likely harmful consequences. A quality-of-character-utilitarian will argue further that it will be best to develop an attitude in oneself such that adultery is never a serious option. For the circumstances in which the question of adultery may arise are likely to be ones in which we are in no fit condition to weigh up the likely consequences, because we are blinded by passion. A utilitarian may then condemn an act of adultery, even though it was in fact productive of utility, on the grounds that the agent has thereby displayed a faulty character – adultery should never have been considered.

Quality-of-character-utilitarianism may be successful in meeting at least some of the problems utilitarians face in connection with justice. It is by no means obvious, however, that it adequately accounts for our intuitions in the case of Prunella, the prosecutor. For her character failings will not, in fact, lead to bad consequences in the future (recall that she is on the point of retirement). So while utilitarians can condemn her for having failed to become the sort of person she should have become, they still have no basis for condemning her action in this case. On the contrary, they still seem committed to the unpalatable conclusion that her action is, in the circumstances, the right one. Moreover, it is, in any case, doubtful whether there will always be appropriate qualities of character to hand, to reconcile utilitarianism with common-sense judgement. For example, in the case of Daniel, the doctor, discussed earlier, what weakness of character would be displayed if he were to use the drug to cure many cases of acne rather than to save a life? The only plausible candidate is his very preparedness to weigh up minor benefits to many people against major harm to an individual. But then it seems we cannot, in utilitarian terms, explain why this would be a bad attitude to have – on the contrary, it is just what utilitarians think we ought to do.

THE DEMANDS OF MORALITY

The move to quality-of-character-utilitarianism is also powerless in the face of the other main charge made against utilitarianism – that it is too demanding. Notice, to begin with, that an act-utilitarian holds that there is only one duty, that is binding at all times, namely to maximise utility. But it seems, intuitively, to be too much to ask that I should run around doing good all the time. There must surely be some private space left to me, in which I can be free to pursue my own projects, and attend to my own interests and the interests of those whom I love.

There are, in fact, two rather different objections here, that are not often distinguished from one another, one theoretical and one practical. The theoretical objection is that utilitarianism is committed to a twofold classification of actions into those that are duties (morally required of us) and those that are against duty (morally forbidden) – at least if we ignore those rare cases where there may be a tie between two incompatible actions in our assessments of overall utility. (In such cases our obligation is only to perform one or other of these actions, rather than either in particular.) Our ordinary moral thought, in contrast, classifies actions threefold, into those that are duties, those that are against duty, and those that are neither. We tend to think that there is a non-moral space left to us (perhaps an extensive one), within which we are free to do what we wish, provided that we do nothing wrong. When I relax in front of the TV in the evening, for example, I am (often) neither performing a duty nor doing anything wrong. This non-moral space is lost to us under utilitarianism.

(Note that the standard utilitarian response to the practical objection, to be considered in a moment – that the greatest utility will in fact be produced if people generally attend to their own happiness and the happiness of those close to them – is no response at all to the current theoretical objection. For it does not deliver the desired conclusion that I am often morally *free* to do what I want, but only that it is often my moral *duty* to do what I want, in so far as doing what I want will in fact be productive of the greatest utility.)

There is a related theoretical point to this one. It is that utilitarianism, of whatever variety, is incapable of drawing a distinction between obligation and saintliness (or between duty and what is beyond duty). Since we are obliged to act for the best (or to follow rules, or develop qualities of character that will be productive of the best) it is impossible, on utilitarian grounds, to do more than one ought to. Yet our common-sense morality certainly includes the idea that there are actions and qualities of character that are supererogatory – above and beyond the call of duty.

One possible response to this difficulty would be to shift to a version of utilitarianism that would require us only to seek *satisfactory* consequences, rather than the best.[3] But this would then lose touch with the governing conception of the theory. It is impossible to see why an impartial benevolent observer should accept a satisfactory outcome, rather than the best. For selecting a situation that is sub-optimal would generally mean that at least some of the claims and interests of some people would have been ignored. Moreover, even this version of utilitarianism will not reinstate our threefold moral classification of actions. It will only mean that there are many more cases where I can fulfil my duty by performing any one of a range of actions, each of which would have satisfactory consequences. This is still not the conclusion we want, that there are many circumstances in which I have no duties at all.

The practical objection to utilitarianism is that, even setting aside the above theoretical considerations, utilitarians are committed to claiming that I must be constantly at work in the service of others, which seems, from a common-sense perspective, to be too much to ask. The reply to this difficulty has generally been to argue that the greatest utility will in fact be produced if people mostly attend to their own happiness, and the happiness of those who are close to them, whose desires and needs they know best. For it is easy to get the desires of strangers badly wrong, and one may readily make mistakes in promoting remote consequences. This is the suggestion that one should develop in oneself an attitude of restricted attention, and it is thus, in effect, a move towards quality-of-character-utilitarianism. The idea is that, in general, one should pay attention to the happiness of those close by, only considering the utility of strangers when the situation demands it. Now this reply might have considerable plausibility in a world where all are roughly equally well off. But in a very unequal world, such as ours, any given quantity of money or time spent in pursuit of utility will be of much more value to those who have least – a crust of bread may mean nothing to me, but may mean everything to one who is starving. Moreover, in the case of extreme suffering there seems to be no special problem in knowing what people want – they want food, shelter, warmth, and peace. It looks, then, as if in our world the difficulty remains – a utilitarian must claim that I should give up all (or almost all) for the sake of beneficence.[4]

It is hard to estimate the precise force of the current –

practical – objection to utilitarianism. For utilitarians can claim that the old morality is the morality of complacency and selfishness. Indeed, the considerations above suggest that the only option for utilitarians is to concede that on this matter they are out to reform common-sense morality, rather than to accommodate it. My own view is that the resulting position is highly implausible, especially when it can be contrasted with a form of contractualism that would require me to develop dispositions towards beneficence sufficient to account for my fair share of alleviating suffering (but no more), and which also allows for a private space that is outside the moral sphere altogether. But I recognise that this is not a matter that admits of decisive proof.

I conclude that while utilitarianism has its advantages, it also has very considerable drawbacks. We might be well advised to seek some alternative theoretical framework if we can. With this in mind, I shall now turn to consider contractualist approaches to morality.

VARIETIES OF CONTRACTUALISM

Contractualism is named after its governing conception, which views morality as the result of an imaginary contract between rational agents, who are agreeing upon rules to govern their subsequent behaviour. It needs to be stressed that the contract in question is hypothetical, not actual. The idea is not that moral rules have resulted from some explicit contract entered into by human beings in an earlier historical era, a claim that is almost certainly false. (John Locke seems to have held a view of this sort.)[5] Nor is the idea that we are, now, implicitly committed to a contract of the 'I won't hit you if you don't hit me' variety, which implausibly reduces moral motivation to self-interest. (This was the position of Thomas Hobbes.)[6] While there have been versions of contractualist moral theory of these sorts, this is not the way in which I propose to use the term in this book. A contractualist moral theory, as I shall understand it, is an attempt to justify a system of moral principles by showing that they *would* be agreed upon by rational agents in certain ideal

circumstances. It is an attempt to exhibit the rationality of
moral rules, not an attempt to legitimate those rules by appeal
to past agreement or present self-interest.

What all the different varieties of contractualism have in
common is that they deem morality to be a human construction,
created by human beings in order to govern their relationships
with one another in society. Contractualism, too, can thus avoid
all the difficulties that attend strong objectivism and intuitionism as theories of ethics. Moral values are not regarded as being
'out there' in the world, any more than the difference between
spices and other foodstuffs is, except in the innocuous sense that
human beings have created a conceptual system that puts them
there. All the same, most contractualists have thought that
moral rules are imposed upon us, in one way or another, by our
very rationality. So moral rules may be held to be objective, not
just in the weak objectivist sense that, given a system of moral
concepts, there are then objective truths about what one may or
may not do, but also in the stronger sense that we cannot, in so
far as we are rational, select an alternative system of concepts.
But since it goes without saying that human beings do not
always behave or choose rationally, all versions of contractualism employ some variant on the idea of an imaginary contract,
so as to idealise away from our limited rationality, and to
represent what we would choose if we were perfectly rational.

The main historical exponent of contractualism, in my sense,
was Immanuel Kant.[7] He regarded morality as arising out of a
process of rational construction, moral rules being those that
rational agents could not rationally wish to be universally
ignored. On this account, the rule 'Do not kill for gain' is a
moral one because you cannot rationally want a society in
which all are prepared to kill for gain. While there is no explicit
mention of a contract here, still the distinctive feature of
Kantian moral construction is that agents should be seeking
rules that all can rationally agree to. (Kant would say that their
very rationality requires them to seek such rules, but that is
another matter.) Kant's own formulations give rise to many
technical and interpretative difficulties, however, and are
embedded within theories of human nature and the origin of

knowledge that are highly controversial. Accordingly, I shall confine my discussion of contractualism to some more recent theoretical work that can, nevertheless, be described as 'Kantian', in that it continues to see morality as arising out of a process of rational construction by rational agents.

Undoubtedly the most famous and influential contemporary version of contractualism is that presented and defended by John Rawls in *A Theory of Justice*. Since Rawls is mainly interested in political philosophy, his application of the contract idea is primarily to determine the basic institutions and structures of a just society. But I propose that we may deploy his version of contractualism for the wider purpose of constructing a general theory of morality. The basic idea, then, is that we are to think of morality as the rules that would be selected by rational agents choosing from behind what Rawls calls *a veil of ignorance*. While these agents may be supposed to have knowledge of all general truths of psychology, sociology, economics, and so on, they are to be ignorant of their own particular qualities (their intelligence, physical strength, qualities of character, projects, and desires), as well as the position they will occupy in the society that results from their choice of rules.

No real person could ever be in such a position, of course, nor is Rawls committed to claiming that they could. No one could ever be in ignorance of such basic facts about themselves as their desires, their rough age, or their sex. Yet agents under the veil of ignorance would know none of these things. The point of the restrictions is to eliminate bias and special pleading in the selection of moral principles. Rawls thinks that, since the position behind the veil of ignorance is a fair one (all are equally rational agents, none has any more knowledge than any of the others), the resulting system of morality must also be fair. Hence his proposal is, in fact, that moral rules are those that we would rationally agree to if we were choosing from a position of complete fairness.

Most importantly, the agents behind the veil of ignorance must not be supposed to have, as yet, any moral beliefs. For part of the point of the theory is to explain how moral beliefs can arise. Moreover, since the idea is that we may seek to resolve moral disputes by subjecting the beliefs in question to the test of their derivability from a particular moral theory, we cannot allow moral beliefs themselves to figure within the theory, or all the original disputes will simply replicate themselves at that level also. The choice of moral principles is rather to be made in the light of broadly self-interested desires (such as those for happiness, freedom, and power) that the agents know they will possess whatever particular desires and interests they subsequently come to have. The agents will know that, whatever they want, they will want their most important desires to be satisfied, they will want the freedom to satisfy them, and they will want the power to do so.

Rawls's theory is by no means the only form of contemporary contractualism, although it is certainly the best known, and probably the most thoroughly worked out. Since one of our goals in later chapters will be to see what consequences contractualism *as such* has for the question of the moral standing of animals, it is important that we should consider at least one other formulation of the doctrine. Otherwise we may easily be misled in thinking that we are drawing out the implications of a contractualist approach to ethics, when in reality we may only be tracing out the consequences of Rawls's particular version of it.

I propose, in addition, to consider the version of contractualism that has been developed more recently by Thomas Scanlon.[8] Scanlon acknowledges a debt to Rawls, but thinks his formulation is able to avoid many of the difficulties that have been raised against *A Theory of Justice*. His account of morality is roughly this: moral rules are those that no one could reasonably reject as a basis for free, unforced, general agreement amongst people who share the aim of reaching such an agreement.

The basic picture of morality here is essentially similar to that of Rawls, and would arguably justify many of the same normative principles, as we shall see in the next section. It is much less artificial, however, and it contains many fewer idealisations. For here the agents concerned are supposed to be real ones, with knowledge of their own idiosyncratic desires and interests, and of their position within the current structure of society. The only idealisations are that choices and objections are always rational (whereas real agents are only sometimes rational, often making mistakes), and that all concerned will share the aim of reaching free and unforced agreement (whereas many real agents may seem indifferent to such considerations). Yet, arguably, these idealisations can achieve the same effect as Rawls's veil of ignorance (that is, the elimination of bias and special pleading). For the contractors will know that there is no point in rejecting a proposed rule on grounds special to themselves, since others would then have equal reason to reject *any* proposed rule.

It may be worth noticing how Scanlon's version of contractualism is reminiscent of one of Kant's formulations of the basic moral perspective, namely that it is a 'kingdom of ends'.[9] Kant's picture is of an association of rational agents, each of whom is legislating for all – that is, each of whom is trying to devise principles that could be freely and rationally acceptable to all. This is, in effect, Scanlon's formulation minus the qualification that the agents share the aim of reaching free agreement. Kant would think that the qualification is not needed, because he holds that the basic principles of morality can be derived from reason alone. The only idealisation necessary, for Kant, is that the agents should always decide rationally.

Notice that if Kant's version of contractualism were acceptable, we should have an immediate explanation of the source of moral motivation. For if moral principles can be derived from pure reason, in such a way that immoral action is always at the same time irrational action, then the answer to the question 'Why care about morality?' is plain. It is, that concern with morality is forced upon us, in so far as we are rational. Along with most contemporary thinkers, however, I believe that this aspect of Kant's programme is hopeless.[10] Since there is no prospect of deriving morality from reason alone, Scanlon's qualification – that the agents must share the aim of reaching free agreement – is a necessary one. I shall return in a later section to the question whether contractualism, thus construed, is capable of explaining the source of moral motivation.

THE NORMATIVE OUTPUT OF CONTRACTUALISM

A collection of rational agents choosing moral rules from behind
a veil of ignorance would plausibly agree, most fundamentally,
to respect one another's autonomy. They would agree not to
interfere with one another's projects, except where this is
necessary to prevent a similar interference with their own. Most
importantly, they would agree not to attack or kill one another,
except in self-defence. It seems likely, indeed, that the most
fundamental moral principle under any version of contractualism will be a principle of respect for autonomy – that agents
should be granted as much freedom to act and pursue projects
as is compatible with a similar degree of freedom being granted
to all the others. For given that you do not know, or cannot
legitimately appeal to, your particular strengths, weaknesses, or
life-plans, or your position under the system of rules to be
selected, you will wish to preserve as much space for yourself as
possible. Under these conditions, rational agents may be
expected to value their own rational agency above all else.

Undoubtedly the main attraction of contractualism, for many
thinkers, lies in its basic normative principle. There is a powerful
intuitive appeal in a rule requiring that people should not, so far
as possible, interfere with one another's plans and projects. The
principle of respect for autonomy is attractive in providing
adequate defence for individuals against interference from
other individuals or groups, or, indeed, from the state itself. It
provides the basis for an acceptable set of rules regulating
people's interactions with one another, while at the same time
leaving a substantial domain within which they remain free to
get on with their own lives, and to develop their own concerns
and interests, without direction from morality. Here, then, are
already two significant contrasts with utilitarianism – namely,
that the lives and interests of individuals cannot be interfered
with merely to subserve greater overall utility, and also that our
common-sense belief in non-moral space is preserved.

Rawls himself also argues that contractualism entails a
particular solution to the problem of distributive justice, which
he calls *the difference principle*. Since agents in the original position

are to be ignorant of their place within the structure of the society that will result from their choice of basic rules, there is an initial presumption in favour of equality of distribution of goods and duties. For none will wish to be disadvantaged. They may rationally accept deviations from this basic equality, however, provided that the resulting increase in efficiency leaves the worst-off person under the new system better off. This, then, is the difference principle: differences in wealth and power are only acceptable if those who are worst off under the system are better off than the worst-off people would have been under any alternative system. This normative implication of contractualism, too, strikes many as having a powerful intuitive appeal – although what its implementation would mean in practice, of course, will depend upon highly contentious claims of psychology, economics, and political theory.

In fact, Rawls himself is only able to derive the difference principle, within his system, by disallowing gambling from behind the veil of ignorance. Otherwise the contractors might rationally opt for a highly unequal distribution, provided that their chances of being in the worst-off group were slim. But that gambling should be disallowed has seemed to many to have been a theoretically arbitrary restriction. This is one of those places where Scanlon's version of contractualism may have the advantage, since it arguably entails something similar, at least, to the difference principle. For those who are worst off under a given system of distribution may surely be reasonable in rejecting it, whenever they have *greater* reason to reject that system than those who are better off have reason to reject the alternative.

It is worth noticing, also, that although contractualism is supposed to legitimate a system of rules, it has no difficulty with the sorts of case – such as the judicial punishment of the innocent – that cause such trouble for utilitarianism. For it must be assumed that the moral rules agreed under the contract will be publicly known – it is part of the very ethos of contractualism that rules and practices should be publicly justifiable. (In contrast, utilitarianism need not assume that everyone will be a utilitarian. On the contrary, it should not assume what is false.)

Since contractualism pictures morality as arising out of agreement between rational agents, the resulting rules must be supposed to be known to all. Indeed, close to the heart of the contractualist approach lies an ideal of *publicity* – namely, that moral rules and principles should be publicly negotiable and defensible in open debate. And then rational agents selecting rules to govern their interaction would, of course, choose principles of justice and punishment that are impartial and exceptionless. For it would obviously be intolerable for it to be commonly known that there is a general rule allowing the punishment of the innocent in the service of expediency, since such a rule would undermine confidence in the whole system.

One difficulty that many people see in the normative output of contractualism is that the resulting rules are too minimal and negative. There will, it seems, be rules enjoining us not to interfere, but no rules enjoining us to assist. There will be rules forbidding us from taking lives, but no rules requiring us to save lives. In short, the accusation is that contractualism places all of its emphasis on justice, to the exclusion of beneficence. This is certainly a serious charge. For there are, intuitively, a great many sorts of situation in which one ought to help others. If contractualism must entail that there are no such situations, then it will surely have been shown to be inadequate under reflective equilibrium.

To see how powerful is the case for an obligation of beneficence, consider a dramatic example of Peter Singer's.[11] While Carl is walking to work one day he passes a shallow pond in which he can see that a child is drowning. No one else is around. Surely he ought to wade in to save the child. The only cost to himself is that he will be slightly late for work and that his clothes will become wet and muddy, whereas the gain will be the life of the child, with all that means both to itself and its parents. If Carl chooses to ignore the child's plight, indeed, then this would surely be an extremely serious moral failing – not quite tantamount to murder, perhaps, but almost as bad in its complete callousness. Yet, no principle of non-interference would have been breached. By failing to save the child he could not, by any stretch of the imagination, be said to have interfered with its plans or projects. His failure to save, in these circumstances, is in conflict, not with justice, but with beneficence. So what is a contractualist to say?

I do not believe that there is any special problem for contractualism here, in fact. While it is true that contractualists have tended to devote most of their time to developing principles of justice, and have talked largely about rights to non-interference rather than obligations to render assistance, this seems to me to have been an accident. It just so happens that this is the area of morality in which contractualists have been most interested. Partly, no doubt, this is because the differences between contractualism and utilitarianism are at their greatest at this point, as we have just seen. For what could be more natural than to place most emphasis upon those aspects of your theory that differentiate it from its main rival? I propose to postpone to Chapter 7 the task of showing in detail how contractualism can accommodate principles of beneficence. But the basic idea is simply that contracting agents should, if they are rational, agree to develop in themselves an attachment to the welfare of others, of sufficient strength to ensure that they do their fair share in alleviating suffering. So callous Carl may be severely criticised for failing in this regard, even though he infringes no one's rights.

THE GOVERNING CONCEPTION OF CONTRACTUALISM

If it is true that contractualism can account for duties of assistance as well as those of non-interference, then at this stage in our investigation it begins to seem likely that contractualism can meet one of the main constraints placed upon the adequacy of a moral theory, namely that it should have a normative output that is, by and large, intuitively acceptable. But what of the other main constraint, that an acceptable moral theory should provide a plausible account of the source of moral notions, and of the basis of moral motivation? Let us take these in turn.

Contractualism certainly suggests a plausible theory of how morality can come to exist at all. As we saw earlier, moral notions are presented as human constructions that arise in order to facilitate human co-operation and the life of community. In any actual society, of course, many different forces and pressures will have shaped the structure of its morality. Contractualism presents us with a way of seeing what our morality should be, if the only constraints on its content are rational ones.

Now consider what contractualism can say about the source of moral motivation. This seems much more problematic. For why should we be interested in what rational agents would choose from behind a veil of ignorance, for example? Why would this be something worth dying for, in the way that many have laid down their lives in the service of justice? Indeed, why should we ourselves feel constrained by what rational agents would agree from behind the veil? Why do *I* have any reason to accept the rules that *they* would accept? Rawls provides a partial answer to these questions in terms of the notion of fairness – since the position behind the veil is fair, it is guaranteed that rational choice from such a position will be fair. Although helpful, in the end this just pushes the problem further back. For why are we interested in fairness? What is the source of our motivation towards arrangements that are fair? Until these questions are answered, contractualism has not really justified its governing conception.

One approach, implicit in some of Rawls's later writings, might be to maintain that we care about morality, as contractualism pictures it, because without it there can be no lasting and non-violent solutions to areas of social conflict, given the basic nature of modern society.[12] Since we can no longer appeal to theological authority to resolve moral disputes, and since no body of traditional belief can now hope to secure universal assent, the only way in which we can have a chance of achieving moral consensus is through reasoned agreement. This explains the source of moral motivation *for us*, living as we do in pluralistic and relatively free societies. But even those traditional societies that still remain might have reason to accept the need for rationally agreed rules and principles, since the nature of our modern world is such that all communities must necessarily interpenetrate one another to some degree.

Another approach, defended by Scanlon, maintains that the solution to the motivation problem is simply to postulate that human beings have a basic need to justify their actions to one another in terms that others may freely and rationally accept.[13] That human beings do have such a need is certainly very plausible. Even scoundrels will characteristically attempt some such justification for what they do. As Scanlon remarks, the notorious difficulty of motivating people to do the right thing need not result from any deficiency in their underlying moral motive, but rather from the ease with which it is deflected by self-interest and self-deception.

Scanlon supposes that the requisite desire to justify oneself is produced and nurtured by moral education. I think it might more plausibly be maintained that it is innate (inborn), in such a way as to emerge gradually at a given stage in maturational development. The case for believing that a good deal of human cognition is innate, including knowledge of the basic principles of human psychology, is a powerful one.[14] What more natural, then, than that the basic springs of characteristic human motivations (including moral motivation) should be innate also? Certainly one would expect such an innate feature of human beings to have considerable survival value, given that we depend crucially for our survival upon co-operative modes of living.

If the desire to be able to justify oneself to others in terms that they may freely and rationally accept were innate, however, one would certainly expect it to be universal. Yet, it may be objected, there have been many communities in the course of human history that have not conceived of their morality in anything like contractualist terms. We may note in reply that what someone may rationally accept will depend, in part, upon their background beliefs. If you believe that the world is ruled by a benevolent and just God, for example, who watches over us as his children and who wishes us to arrange our lives along the hierarchical lines of feudal societies, then you might freely and rationally accept the rules that assign you your role as a serf in such a society.

Once again an analogy with other areas of our cognition may

prove helpful. There is a powerful case for saying that the basic principles we employ in justifying our beliefs about the world – particularly inference to the best explanation of a given phenomenon – are innate.[15] Yet what counts as the best explanation of something is, in part, a function of the other beliefs that you hold, since one feature of a good explanation is that it should cohere well with surrounding beliefs and theories.[16] This enables us to discern an underlying unity beneath the very different sorts of explanations that may be preferred within different human communities. I am suggesting something similar in connection with the manifest diversity in human moralities – that they may reflect the same (innate) underlying conception of moral justification, put to work in the context of different social practices and metaphysical beliefs. My hypothesis is thus that the contractualist concept may form the core of all the different moralities that human beings have endorsed. At any rate, this is sufficiently plausible to make contractualism, when taken together with the appeal of its normative output, a very strong contender overall for the title of most acceptable moral theory. But we have yet to consider some powerful criticisms that have been levelled against the theory.

REPLIES TO CRITICISMS

One criticism of contractualism is that it is parochial – that it merely expresses the values of liberal capitalist democracies. One aspect of this charge is easy to rebut, namely the commitment to capitalism. Whether or not contractualists should be capitalists will depend upon the facts of economics and psychology necessary to apply the difference principle. If it were true, as socialists generally claim, that socialist economies serve to unleash the forces of production, leading to better living standards for all, as well as to greater control by individuals over the course of their own lives, then it would be socialism that should be selected. It is just that many contractualists doubt whether these claims are true.

The commitment to liberal democracy, however, seems to go

deeper. Rawls, indeed, is happy to accept this commitment, and the associated charge of parochialism, claiming it as a positive virtue.[17] He regards the apparatus of the veil of ignorance as modelling the values implicit in liberal democracies, rather than as providing an account of universal morality as such. It is merely a device to enable us to gain a clearer self-image, and to work out the consequences of our most fundamental values. If the suggestions I made in the last section were on the right lines, however, then Rawls may have been too pessimistic about the prospects for contractualism to serve as the universal morality. If the contractualist conception is innate to human beings, then liberal democracy may merely be what you get once morality is stripped of its connections with religious belief, and of its association with such beliefs as that ill-educated people, women, and members of other races are not properly rational agents, needing in important respects to be treated as children.

While some have charged contractualism with parochialism, others have levelled the opposite – communitarian – charge against it. They have claimed that in aiming to be universal it has become too abstract, breaking the connection between moral values and the communities and practices in which they are embedded.[18] But this is to miss the point made above, that what rules it may be rational to accept or reject will depend, in part, upon the other beliefs and values current in the community. We should, therefore, expect a good deal of cultural variation in the way that contractualism gets embodied in concrete institutions and practices. Moreover, as Scanlon points out, there may be a number of different sets of principles that pass the contractualist test of non-rejectability, and yet any moral community will need to settle upon one from amongst the options available.[19] (Compare: while there are no theoretical considerations that determine whether we should drive our cars on the right or the left, we plainly need to settle upon one or other of these in particular.) Contractualism would then entail that many obligations and duties are to be established by convention, and may therefore vary from society to society.

The above objection can be restated in a stronger form, however. It can be claimed that the apparatus of the veil of ignorance entails that rational agents can exist prior to possessing any particular set of desires and values, having an identity that is independent of them. Whereas, it may be said, such agents are always, and essentially, members of some moral community. Indeed, the very identities of those agents may be tied to the values and practices which form a necessary part of the communities that have nurtured and shaped them. But in my view, contractualism carries no such presupposition about the identities of persons. All that it presupposes is something much weaker and more plausible, namely that it is possible for rational agents, in some of their reasonings, to bracket off even those values and concerns that contribute to their identities, subjecting those values to examination and possible criticism from a more abstract perspective. Even if my sense of loyalty as a feudal serf forms a necessary part of who I am, as an individual, it is surely possible, temporarily setting those loyalties to one side, that I should raise the question whether feudal institutions might reasonably be rejected by those seeking to agree on moral rules. It is also possible that I might arrive at a negative verdict, and that I should, in consequence, come to change my moral commitments, and hence my own identity as a person.

My conclusion is that the communitarian challenge to contractualism fails. So we are left with a theory whose governing conception is at least as plausible as that of utilitarianism, but whose normative output is considerably more attractive.

SUMMARY

I have developed versions of both utilitarianism and contractualism that can claim not only to present a satisfying explanation of the origins of morality and of moral motivation, but also to accommodate a good deal, at least, of common-sense moral judgement. My own view is that contractualism is, under reflective equilibrium, by far the more plausible moral theory.

But both are sufficiently powerful that we shall need to consider the consequences of each of them for our treatment of animals. It will be a further test of the adequacy of our two candidate theories that they should entail acceptable consequences on such matters.

CHAPTER 3

Utilitarianism and animal suffering

In this chapter I shall begin considering what a utilitarian should say about the moral standing of animals. I shall confine my attention to the question of the moral standing of animal experience (particularly pleasure and pain), reserving to Chapter 4 discussion of utilitarian approaches to the value of animal life.

RACISM, SEXISM, AND SPECIESISM

Peter Singer has been prominent in arguing for the moral standing of animals and animal suffering, through such books as *Animal Liberation*[1] and *Practical Ethics*. He does not, in fact, explicitly premise his argument on any version of utilitarianism. For he wants that argument to be acceptable to all, whatever their theoretical standpoint. His strategy here is a good one. Any moral argument will be the stronger for being able to survive translation between ethical theories, being equally stateable in a variety of them. I shall show later that Singer's argument is only really acceptable from a utilitarian standpoint, however – in particular, that it has no force against a contractualist.

Singer's argument starts from a principle of equal consideration of interests. This holds that in any situation the interests of all those affected should be considered equally, which may sound, on the face of it, like a utilitarian principle. But in fact Singer is correct that, suitably interpreted, it should be equally acceptable to contractualists. For contracting agents may reasonably reject any rule that gives their interests no weight, or that treats those interests as having less significance than those of other agents, as we shall see in Chapter 5. It seems plain, in contrast, that no one could reasonably reject a rule requiring us to treat everyone's interests as of equal weight – which is the principle of equal consideration of interests.

To say that everyone's interests should be given equal consideration is not to say, of course, (for a contractualist at least) that everyone's interests should be *met* equally. Much will depend upon the circumstances. If some of us have freely agreed to pay money into a lottery, for example, then only those who have contributed may be considered for a prize. This does not conflict with the principle of equal consideration, since the others are not discriminated against – they were free to take part if they wished. What would genuinely conflict with the principle of equal consideration would be, for example, a policy of only considering for prizes those with white skins, whether or not they have contributed to the lottery.

Singer's explanation of the immorality of both racism and sexism is that these practices violate the principle of equal consideration. For example, the policies of the South African government through most of the decades of this century have counted white interests as worth a lot, and the interests of blacks and coloureds as being comparatively much less significant. Similarly, the policies of many governments and individuals around the globe treat the interests of women as worth less than those of men. These policies are wrong, and count as violating the principle of equal consideration, because the characteristics of skin colour and sex are morally irrelevant ones. While the fact of having contributed money to a lottery is morally relevant when it comes to the distribution of prizes, the fact of having white skin, or being male, is plainly not. Indeed, there are hardly any important contexts in which these latter features could be morally relevant. (Exceptions might be the distribution of creams to prevent skin cancer in whites, and screening for testicular cancer in men.)

Singer's main argument is then that speciesism, like racism and sexism, is wrong because it discriminates on the basis of morally irrelevant characteristics. To give lesser, or no, weight to the interests of animals violates the principle of equal consideration because such a policy must be grounded in either the mere differences of species between animals and ourselves, or in the differences of appearance, or in the differences of intelligence. Yet none of these characteristics is morally relevant, Singer argues. Let us discuss each of them in turn.

It seems plain that species membership is a morally irrelevant characteristic. Two examples will suffice to make the point. First, suppose that the experiments attempting to teach language to chimpanzees had been successful beyond their originators wildest dreams. The apes in question gained a complete mastery of English within a few years, were able to attend school and later university, and made many close friendships with human beings. In these imaginary circumstances it would plainly be absurd to claim that the apes lacked moral standing, or had a moral importance that was lower than our own. At any rate, to make these claims would plainly be morally objectionable in exactly the way that similar claims made about members of different races are morally objectionable. So species membership, in itself, cannot be a morally relevant characteristic, serving to justify differential treatment of animals.

Consider a second example to make the same point. It is well known that about 10 per cent of human couples are infertile. Then suppose it had been discovered that the reason for this is that human beings in fact consist of two distinct species, otherwise hardly distinguishable from one another, the members of which cannot inter-breed. In these circumstances it would plainly be objectionable for the members of the majority species to attempt to withhold moral rights from the members of the minority, on the mere ground of difference of species. This, too, would be obvious speciesism.

Now consider two examples to make the point that differences of appearance between humans and animals cannot serve as a moral ground for differential treatment of the latter. First, consider human beings who have been victims of the drug Thalidomide, taken by their mothers during early pregnancy. These people often appear very different from normal humans, with perhaps no legs and just a few fingers sprouting from a shoulder. But that is plainly no ground for treating their interests as being lesser than our own. Second, suppose that there were to be radiation victims following a nuclear accident who, while otherwise normal human beings, were born covered with thick dark fur like monkeys. Again, these people's difference in appearance from ourselves would plainly be no ground for refusing to count them equally.

Finally, consider two examples to make essentially the same point in connection with differences of intelligence between animals and ourselves. Suppose that doctors with a limited supply of kidney dialysis machines were to begin intelligence-testing their kidney patients, only offering treatment to those scoring above a certain level. Would there not be an immediate moral outcry, and rightly so? It is plainly morally repugnant to make life-or-death decisions on the basis of intelligence. Similarly, suppose that a cosmetics company were to begin testing their products in a home for severely retarded children, using the same painful experiments currently employed on animals to ensure that their products are safe. Again, the outcry would be immediate. The sufferings of those children could not be ignored merely on the grounds that the children are of lower intelligence than ourselves.

The conclusion Singer draws from considerations of this sort is that it is morally indefensible to exclude animals from the scope of the principle of equal consideration of interests.[2] Since the various characteristics that distinguish us from animals – that is, species, appearance, and intelligence – are morally irrelevant, animal interests should be counted equally with our own. Pain is pain, no matter who feels it, and is just as morally significant. I shall shortly discuss one of the presuppositions of Singer's position – that animals do genuinely have interests to be considered – and what the practical consequences of his conclusion would be. But first I shall dig a little deeper into the notion of a morally relevant characteristic.

THE RELATIVITY OF RELEVANCE

My first thesis is a general one, that relevance is always relative to a point of view. Imagine that Tania and Teresa are watching a tennis game, and are asked whether or not it is relevant who wins. Tania might reply that it is not, since she just likes to watch good tennis. Teresa, on the other hand, might reply that it is, since she has a substantial bet riding on the outcome of the game. What is relevant to the one is irrelevant to the other, in virtue of the different perspectives that they take towards the game – the different kinds of interest that they have in it. So, when it is claimed that species membership is a morally irrelevant characteristic, we need to know the point of view being taken, in order to assess the claim. That is, we need to know how the moral point of view is being characterised. Once the matter is viewed in this light, it can be seen that Singer's argument is, in fact, only sound from the standpoint of a utilitarian conception of morality.

Given a contractualist conception of the moral point of view, intelligence – or at least a certain kind and level of intelligence – is not morally irrelevant, as we shall see in Chapter 5. On the contrary, for a contractualist it will turn out to be a sufficient condition for a creature to have moral standing that it should be a rational agent, and this is, broadly, a matter of its intelligence. This explains the appeal of many of the examples used above, such as the example of the English-speaking apes, and the examples of the Thalidomide and radiation victims. For in each case it is plain that the individuals in question are rational agents. To say that rational agency is morally relevant under contractualism, however, is not to say that differences of intelligence amongst rational agents must also have moral relevance. On the contrary, one would expect rational contractors to outlaw discrimination on the basis of such differences, of the kind involved in the example of the kidney dialysis machines discussed above. For those who are of lower intelligence might surely be reasonable in rejecting any rules that allow their interests to be discounted, or counted for less.

It is also the case that species membership, together with the

similarities of appearance and patterns of behaviour with which
it is associated, is not morally irrelevant under contractualism
– at least if the arguments to be presented in Chapters 5 and 7
are sound. There I shall argue that rational contractors should
extend direct moral rights to all members of the human species,
in order to avoid the dangers of a slippery slope and to preserve
social stability, and in order not to undermine our natural
reactions of sympathy for human suffering. Since these arguments do not support the extension of direct moral rights to
members of other species, it will turn out that species membership is a morally relevant characteristic from the perspective
of contractualism.

From this discussion it emerges that what really drives
Singer's argument is a particular conception of the moral point
of view, which identifies it with the standpoint of an impartial
benevolent observer, who is equally sympathetic to the interests
of all who are affected by a given action or situation.[3] It also
emerges that there is *nothing* really driving Regan's argument in
The Case for Animal Rights, which makes similar claims about the
moral irrelevance of species membership and intelligence.[4] For
as we saw in Chapter 1, Regan fails altogether to provide us
with a characterisation of the moral point of view, relying
entirely, as he does, on his – restricted – understanding of
reflective equilibrium to establish his views. Since we lack such
a characterisation, we lack the means necessary to assess his
claims about moral relevance.

The standpoint of the impartial benevolent observer is, you
will recall from the last chapter, the governing conception of
utilitarianism, which regards moral concerns as arising out of
rationalised (impartial) sympathy. It is certainly true that there
can be no reason why an impartial observer should count
animal interests as of lower importance than our own. It is also
true that rational agency and species membership are both
morally irrelevant, from the standpoint of such an observer.
The only relevant features are the capacity for pain and
pleasure, as well as the capacity for desire. Under utilitarianism
the boundaries of moral concern are co-extensive with the
boundaries of sentience – that is to say, with the capacity for

experience. If an animal can suffer, then, plainly, it may be said to have an interest in avoiding suffering. (Even if you think that to have an interest in something implies, strictly speaking, a desire for that thing, this point will still hold. For the very idea of pain seems conceptually tied to the desire for its avoidance. If an animal can suffer at all then it must have at least this one desire.) The principle of equal consideration of interests will then require us to show equal respect for the sufferings and frustrations of every sentient creature.

Singer's argument for extending the principle of equal consideration of interests to animals is therefore less powerful than he would have liked. In particular, that argument can have no force against someone who is already a convinced contractualist. It is, indeed, an argument from the standpoint of utilitarianism. What we are, therefore, investigating is what a utilitarian should say on the subject of the moral standing of animal experience.

DO ANIMALS HAVE INTERESTS?

What a utilitarian (or, indeed, anyone else) should say on this subject is partly dependent upon the facts. I have been assuming, thus far, that animals do have experiences and at least some desires. In which case, the only issue arising when we consider whether the principle of equal consideration of interests should be applied to animals is the moral one. But many have denied this. Many philosophers and psychologists have held that animals are biological automata, lacking mental lives, and engaging in their characteristic behaviours out of acquired habit or innately determined action sequences, rather than because of anything resembling genuine cognition.

There is no doubt that some animals are, in the relevant sense, automata, despite their apparent sentience. When caterpillars hatch from their cocoons, for example, they will climb to the tops of trees to eat the leaves at the tips of the branches. But this apparently purposive behaviour is, in fact, a *tropism* – a mechanical feedback process of a very simple sort. The caterpillars have two eyes, symmetrically positioned on their heads. When the same amount of light enters each of the eyes the caterpillars move straight ahead. But when more light enters one of the eyes the legs on that side of the body move more slowly. The result is that the caterpillars move towards the light. In experiments where the trees were artificially lit from below, the caterpillars moved to the bottom of the trees, where they remained even when starving. When a caterpillar was blinded in one eye it would move endlessly in a circle, again to the point of starving.[5]

Caterpillars will also wriggle vigorously when impaled on the end of a pin. It seems highly likely that this, too, is a simple tropism. Although it might appear to a human observer that the caterpillar is in pain, and is wriggling in an attempt to avoid the source of the pain, in reality it is likely that the nerves sensitive to the presence of the pin feed directly into the muscles responsible for the subsequent movement, without any intervening cognition. Compare this case: you are present at a medical examination of your daughter Patricia, and you observe the doctor tap her on the knee with a hammer, upon which Patricia kicks out her leg. An untutored observer might conclude that Patricia had tried to kick the doctor because she felt pain at the blow. But you would know that it was, in fact, a mere reflex. So, too, I suggest, in the case of the caterpillar.

It seems unlikely that insects are genuinely sentient, in the sense of having mental lives that would include sensations and desires. It is worth noting that this is already to undermine one aspect of common-sense belief. Children who pull the wings off flies, or the legs off ants, are told that it is cruel, and to desist. In most cases their actions are presumably believed to be instances of what Regan calls brutal cruelty (as opposed to sadistic cruelty)[6] – that is, actions that display indifference to the suffering caused to others. Yet these beliefs are false, if insects are not genuinely sentient. Once we realise that insects feel no pain, the only remaining motive for discouraging the children is that their activities are a sort of play-acting for real cruelty. But, in fact, it would be equally effective to teach children to distinguish between sentient and non-sentient creatures – supposing, at least, that the distinction were known.

What, then, are the boundaries of sentience? What sorts of creature are genuinely capable of having pains and other experiences, and of having beliefs and desires? I shall concentrate on the capacity for experience here, returning to the question of animal beliefs and desires in Chapter 6. It seems safe to assume that all mammals, at least, are genuinely sentient, given the variety and flexibility of mammalian behaviours, and given the close similarities in brain structure and function between even the lower mammals and ourselves.[7] A variety of types of evidence also suggests that birds should be classed together with mammals in respect of levels and degree of cognitive organisation, and in contrast with lower vertebrates such as fish, amphibians, and reptiles.[8] At any rate, this is what I propose to assume – that all mammals and birds are genuinely sentient, but that no insects are. For present purposes, I shall remain agnostic about the mental lives of lower vertebrates, since we have already done enough to settle most of the cases relevant to the morally contentious practices of hunting, farming, and animal experimentation. I shall assume that in all such cases involving mammals and birds the animals can experience pain, and thus do genuinely have interests to be considered.

MINDS AND BRAINS

Many of those who have maintained that human beings are unique in the animal kingdom in possessing mental lives have done so, in part, because they have denied that mental events and (some) brain events are one and the same.[9] These people have either held that humans have non-physical souls, which form the true locus of their thoughts and feelings, or they have believed, at any rate, that mental events are non-physical ones, partly caused by and partly causing brain activity. Such people will then be unmoved by the manifest similarities of structure and function between the brains of humans and higher vertebrates.

It is not strictly necessary that we should reject the doctrine of mental immaterialism in order to maintain that higher vertebrates have genuine mental lives. For we could hold that the considerable similarities in behaviour between such animals and human beings would warrant ascribing non-material mental events to both. But our case will be that much stronger if we can also argue, as mental materialists, that the similarities between our brains suggest corresponding similarities in cognition. It is, therefore, worth indicating briefly why I hold that the thesis of mental immaterialism is false.

There are two main arguments for maintaining that our mental lives must consist of physical events in our brains. Both are premised on the common-sense belief that mental events and brain events interact causally with one another. We believe, for example, that retinal stimulation causes certain brain events that cause in us visual sensations in turn, and that mental events such as decisions cause bodily movements that have certain brain events as their immediate causes.

The first argument against mental immaterialism is that, if mental events are non-physical, then we shall be required to recognise a whole new species of causality, hitherto unknown to science. All the types of causal relationship that science has given us reason to believe in – chemical, electrical, mechanical, and so on – relate different classes of physical event. Indeed, it can be said that the distinctive feature of scientific progress over the last three centuries has been the assumption that there will be some sort of physical mechanism underlying any causal relationship. Science really began to make advances when people ceased to offer explanations in terms of causation by spirits and other non-physical forces, and began to hunt for physical mechanisms underlying the observed regularities in nature. The immense success of science then gives us reason to extend this policy into the domain of the mind until proved otherwise. But in fact, far from there being any proof of mental immaterialism, the arguments for it are relatively weak.[10]

The second main argument against mental immaterialism, and in favour of identifying mental events with physical ones, is that enough is already known about the brain for us to be confident that each brain event will have a sufficient physical cause. We know that the human brain is made up of nerve cells, and quite a lot is known about the causes of nerve cell activity. All of these causes are physical ones, including chemical changes in the blood stream, as well as the physical activation of connected cells. Given that this is so, there is then no room for mental events (such as decisions) to cause brain events (in this case the immediate causes in the brain of bodily movements) unless mental events can be identified with the relevant brain events. If decisions (and other mental events) can be causes of bodily movements, then decisions must be brain events. For we know that bodily movements are caused by brain events, each of which, in turn, has a sufficient physical cause.

It is worth emphasising in conclusion of this section that mental materialism has nothing whatever to do with materialism as a system of values. Nothing in what has been said here commits us to the claim that the only things worth caring about are wealth, power, and physical comfort. Nor need there be anything here that is inconsistent with theological beliefs in life after death. For it is possible to believe in resurrection of the body, as many Christians have, in fact, done. Indeed, there might also be other forms of after-life available for a mental materialist to believe in.[11]

COMPARISONS OF INTEREST

I have been arguing that members of many other species of animal, at least, should be counted as having interests, because they are capable of experiencing pain. But what does the principle of equal consideration of interests amount to, where the interests to be considered may cross species boundaries? Are such comparisons of interest even so much as possible? Similar worries to these can, in fact, be raised in connection with comparisons of human interests. For it is possible to doubt whether we can ever know the extent to which other people are really suffering, or even whether they are suffering at all. But this is just the philosophical problem of knowledge of other minds, raised for the particular case of knowledge of other people's experiences. Although this problem may be a theoretically interesting one, few doubt that it must have a solution.[12] That is to say, few are genuinely sceptical of our ability to have knowledge of the mental states of other persons, based on our observations of their behaviour.

If this is so, then it would seem that essentially the same basis must exist for knowledge of the mental states of animals. It is true that in connection with the mental states of human beings we have one additional source of evidence, namely those people's descriptions of the qualities and intensities of their experiences. But it is important to see that this is just one further piece of behavioural evidence, having no special authority. For we still need to make assumptions about the speakers' sincerity and, more importantly, about what they mean by the words that they use. These, in turn, can only be known by means of an inference to the best explanation of the observed patterns in those speakers' behaviour.

There are two different sorts of basis for our judgements of the extent of an animal's suffering. First, we can judge the intensity of that suffering from direct observations of the animal's behaviour – that is, from the degree of the animal's reaction (screaming or howling, for example), and how desperately it tries to avoid the source of the pain. Second, we may judge the intensity of the suffering by making reasonable hypotheses, on the basis of our observation of other similar cases, about what the animal would be prepared to do to avoid the suffering in question. Would it be prepared to endure a painful stimulus like that in order to get food when it is extremely hungry, for example?

Physiological differences between different animal species, of course, and between animals and ourselves, rule out any simple comparisons of suffering. To use an example of Singer's, it is doubtful whether a hard slap to a horse would cause it as much pain as would a similarly hard slap to a human baby. This is because the horse's skin is much thicker than that of the baby. But as Singer correctly says, there must be *some* degree of stimulus that would cause as much pain to the horse as does the slap to the baby.[13] And we would judge this by seeing how the horse reacts – how hard it tries to get away, for example – and by seeing how much the horse would put up with to get something that it really wants, such as water when it is dehydrated.

When considering comparisons of suffering, Singer concedes that levels of intelligence do in fact turn out to be important. In particular, the greater intelligence of most humans gives vastly increased opportunities for suffering. For example, imagine the varied sorts of suffering that would be involved in a policy of random seizures of people off the streets, for use in painful eye-tests of cosmetics. In the first place, of course, there would be the immediate pain of the tests themselves, presumably roughly comparable to the levels of pain experienced by laboratory rabbits. But then, in addition, there would be the fear beforehand, when people know that these seizures are taking place, and when they know exactly what is going to happen to them once they are seized. There would also be the memories remaining afterwards, perhaps with an attendant destruction of the self-esteem of the person in question. For these reasons Singer concedes that if these experiments have to be done at all, then it is better that they should be performed on rabbits than on human beings, since the suffering produced will be less. (He assumes, here, that most animals will lack the sorts of higher mental processes of thought and feeling that give rise to the kinds of additional sufferings mentioned above. I shall grant this assumption for the moment, returning to discuss it in some detail in Chapter 6.) This concession of Singer's is consistent with the principle of equal consideration of interests, since it is only equal suffering that should be considered equally.

PRACTICAL CONSEQUENCES

As we have seen, Singer allows that cross-species comparisons of interests are very difficult to conduct with any degree of accuracy, and that the greater intelligence of most humans vastly increases their capacity for suffering. But he also claims that we only have to be able to make the very roughest of comparisons in order to have an enormous impact on current practices in the treatment of animals. Let us consider in turn the four main categories of hunting, factory farming, cosmetic testing, and medical testing.

People who go hunting often consume the meat of the animals that they kill, and they often wear or sell their skins. But it is arguable that these benefits should not enter into the moral equation at all, since animal pain is not really necessary to provide them. In our modern world meat and furs can be obtained by normal farming, which need involve no suffering for the animals. Such animals can in principle be kept in pleasant conditions throughout their lives before being slaughtered painlessly and unexpectedly. (Recall that the question of the moral standing of animal *lives* is being deferred to Chapter 4.) So, the only relevant advantages to humans from hunting are the pleasures of the hunt itself – tracking, stalking, or chasing an animal, and then trying to kill it. It is in the nature of this activity that it cannot be carried out without frequently causing pain to the animals involved.

Although the pleasures of hunting, for some people, may be considerable, they are surely trivial by comparison with the painful death frequently endured by the animal. If the pain and terror caused by a fatal wound in a deer or rabbit is even roughly comparable to what a human would feel in similar circumstances, then it is obvious that they greatly outweigh any pleasure felt by the hunter. For consider: would even the most dedicated of hunters pursue their sport, if they themselves had to endure suffering comparable to that of each animal they failed to kill cleanly? It seems plain that they would not. In which case, applying the principle of equal consideration of interests here will show hunting to be wrong.

Now consider the practice of factory farming. Here, again, the suffering caused to the animals, through being kept in extremely cramped and unnatural conditions, is considerable. Yet, the only gain to humans is that we should enjoy cheaper (and in some cases, perhaps, tastier) meat. So for each animal that suffers, the proportion of its suffering that is caused by factory farming, throughout the course of its life, has to be set against the marginal pleasures of the dozens of humans who eventually have a share in consuming its flesh. If that animal had not been factory farmed, then the only loss to those people is that they would each have had rather less money to spend on other things.

In this case, too, the application of the principle of equal consideration of interests seems easy. The gains to human beings – even when totalled up – appear trivial when compared with the extensive suffering of the animals. In which case, factory farming will be wrong from the standpoint of a utilitarian. It is important to note, however, that this does not yet justify moral vegetarianism (as opposed, for example, to vegetarianism adopted for reasons of health). For some utilitarians (Singer included) hold the view that while it is wrong to cause animals suffering, it is permissible to kill them painlessly. So farming methods where the animals are kept in enjoyable conditions throughout their lives before being painlessly killed for their meat may turn out to be morally unobjectionable. What utilitarians should say about this will depend on their views on killing in general, and on the value of animal life in particular, which we shall discuss in the next chapter.

The case against cosmetics testing on animals seems equally clear-cut. For the tests are such that the animals in question suffer very severe pain, whereas the gains to humans of being able to use a new cosmetic are marginal. Now it might be replied that in an age of mass-production, even fairly minor pleasures brought to millions of people might easily outweigh the intense sufferings of a few hundred animals. But the pleasures in question are very marginal indeed. For there are already a wide range of cosmetics products in existence. The only cost of banning testing now, would be the loss of the pleasure that some people feel on being able to try something completely new.

There is, however, a point about those who are employed in the cosmetics industry, many of whom might lose their jobs if testing of new products were banned. (This issue does not arise in connection with factory farming, since traditional farming methods are more, rather than less, labour-intensive.) Here the issue is in danger of merging into complex questions of economics and social policy. But as a corrective to it, try to take seriously the application of the principle of equal consideration of interests to animals. For if it were young children rather than animals who were involved, for example, then how many people could seriously place their possession of a job higher than the option of avoiding the suffering that their jobs produce?

Finally, consider the use of animals in painful scientific experiments, particularly those connected with the development and testing of new medicines. This is in many ways the most difficult case, because of the very considerable gains that may result from such experiments, through reducing or avoiding the incidence of painful illnesses in both humans and animals. Might not these benefits outweigh the sufferings of the animals used in the tests? In some cases, surely, they might. But in order to justify any particular series of experiments, we would need to have an assurance that the probability of such benefits accruing is quite high. A mere chance of great benefit will not be enough, when set against the certainty of the suffering caused to the animals involved. In any case, what Singer suggests here as a useful rule of thumb, is that such tests are morally acceptable only if it would be equally acceptable to perform them on mentally retarded orphan humans.[14] (They should be orphans to rule out the question of vicarious suffering caused to parents and relatives.) If this would not be acceptable (as presumably it would not, for most people), then from a utilitarian standpoint it can only be unacceptable speciesism to allow the tests in question to be conducted on animals of similar intelligence.

IS REFLECTIVE EQUILIBRIUM POSSIBLE?

Utilitarianism is clearly committed to making substantial revisions in the common-sense moral beliefs held by most people. It entails (when taken together with reasonable assumptions about the reality of animal experience) that hunting, factory farming, cosmetics testing, and many of the uses of animals in medical experiments are all seriously wrong, and should be stopped. For from the standpoint of the governing conception of utilitarianism – that of an impartial benevolent observer – there can be no reason why the interests of animals should be discounted or outweighed where they conflict with those of human beings. If these consequences are to be acceptable under reflective equilibrium, then we need somehow to explain away the almost universal human belief in their contraries – for example, the belief that the interests of an animal count for practically nothing when set against the suffering of a human being.

Utilitarians have a reply to this difficulty, explaining how it is that most people have had, until now, false beliefs about the extent of the moral significance of animals. For the impartial perspective is by no means an easy one to attain. Indeed, moral progress can be characterised, for a utilitarian, as a constant struggle against our own natural partiality. We are all naturally partial to those who are closest to us, linked to us by ties of blood or affection. Hence the most primitive form of morality is the morality of the clan, withholding moral standing from all outsiders. But reason can gradually modify this partiality, forcing us to recognise that there is no rational basis for counting the interests of those close to us above the interests of other people. In addition, a utilitarian can point out that there have been long periods of human history when an argument for equal consideration of the interests of slaves and slave owners would have struck most people as equally counter-intuitive. So our initial intuitive reaction to the claim that the interests of animals should be counted equally with our own might be claimed to be no more than a product of our natural (but unreasonable) partiality towards members of our own species.

This reply might have been considered adequate, if there had been no other theoretical alternatives available. That is, if we had been faced with a choice between having no coherent theory of morality at all, and one which entailed equal moral standing for animals, it might – perhaps – have been more reasonable to opt for the latter. For similar reasons, the envisaged reply might also have been acceptable if utilitarianism had enjoyed huge theoretical advantages over all alternative moral theories. But these are not, in fact, the choices before us.

For we do have an alternative theory, namely contractualism. This is equally, if not more, theoretically defensible, and can explain the duties towards animals postulated by common-sense morality without granting moral standing to animals, as we shall see in Chapter 7. Given this situation, I propose that the way to achieve reflective equilibrium is to reject utilitarianism altogether, and embrace contractualism instead.

It is worth emphasising that the prohibitions against hunting, factory farming, and laboratory testing on animals are by no means the most counter-intuitive consequences of the utilitarian approach to this issue. Indeed, many ordinary people may hardly find them counter-intuitive at all. Rather, the hardest thing to accept is that the suffering of an animal should have *equal* moral standing with the (equally severe) suffering of a human being. An imaginary example will make the point vivid. Suppose that Saul is a very powerful and evil sadist. You have discovered that in the dungeons of his castle he keeps a number of creatures, including a human being, in conditions of perpetual torture. Now imagine yourself on a rescue mission to his castle. You have somehow discovered a way in, that can only be used once, and you know that you will only have time to release just one of those who are undergoing torture, before the alarm bells start to ring and you are captured yourself.

What should you do? Utilitarianism, being committed to the extension of the principle of equal consideration of interests to animals, entails that, other things being equal, there is nothing to choose – morally speaking, you are free to release any one of the imprisoned creatures at random. Indeed, if one of those creatures were to have a natural life-expectancy greater than that of the human – perhaps an elephant or giant turtle – then a utilitarian might have to claim that you are morally obliged to rescue the animal. These consequences are hugely counter-intuitive. I think most of us would feel that you are under a strong moral obligation to liberate the human being, and that you would, normally, do something very wrong indeed if you chose to save a dog, or an elephant, or a monkey instead.

It is important not to become distracted by irrelevancies at this point. It should be supposed, for example, that you have evidence that is as good as it can be that the degree of suffering of the imprisoned human is no greater than that of the animals. (You may perhaps have had the opportunity to study in detail videotapes of the torture in progress.) Moreover, it should be supposed that you know that the torture of each creature will continue until its natural death, and is of such a severity that it leaves no space in consciousness for any further thought. This is to side-step the point about the additional suffering that the human may later undergo, by re-living the torture in memory, and also the point that the human may suffer additionally through hopelessness and fear of suffering further. Suppose, too, that the human in question is quite old, with a life expectancy no greater than any of the dogs, cats, or monkeys involved. So there is nothing to be gained in the way of additional future happiness by saving the human being. Despite all this, the intuition remains that it would be unforgivable to do anything other than rescue the human being. My view is that this belief is so deeply and firmly held, by most of us, that any moral theory that requires its rejection ought, in turn, to be rejected under reflective equilibrium.

In reply, it may be said that many people have in fact found it quite easy to lose this intuition, and have embraced with enthusiasm the thesis of the equal moral standing of animal suffering, but without especially adopting a utilitarian stand-point. This is true. But so, too, and in the same sense, have people managed to lose their belief in the physical world. In both cases the basic form of the argument is *sceptical*. Those who have lost their belief in physical reality have done so because they doubted whether there is anything that justifies belief in a world of physical objects, given that it is possible for our experiences to be a gigantic hallucination, or to be caused by an evil demon working directly on our minds. Similarly, many of those who have lost their belief in the differential moral standing of human and animal suffering have done so because they doubted whether there is anything that justifies belief in the difference. But, in common with many other philosophers, I believe that scepticism about physical reality is answerable.[15] And it will be the task of Chapters 5 and 7 to answer scepticism about the unequal moral standing of animal suffering. In both cases the sceptical argument is initially attractive (not to say seductive), hard to answer, but ultimately unsound.

Most utilitarians will probably concede that they are in conflict with a key aspect of common-sense moral belief on the issue of animal suffering. But, they may claim, the forces of progress are on their side, in such a way that future generations will judge them, in retrospect, to have been correct. Our current attitudes towards animals, on this analysis, are similar to eighteenth-century attitudes towards slavery and members of 'inferior' races. Indeed, many utilitarians are fond of pointing out that there have been numerous periods of human history in which the extension of the principle of equal consideration of interests to members of other races would have seemed equally counter-intuitive to most ordinary people. Yet we now judge that those people were wrong, and that the minority who protested against such practices as slavery were right.

In fact, however, the two cases are importantly different. For there has never really been a theoretically respectable moral theory that could justify a system of slavery, at least in any of the forms that have actually been practised. (Recall from Chapter 2 that utilitarianism itself may imply that in certain – hypothetical – circumstances an institution of slavery would be justified.) In particular, contractualism, too, entails that slavery was, and is, seriously wrong. Indeed, what more obvious breach could there be of the central contractualist principle of respect for autonomy? What really sustained common-sense beliefs about the permissibility of slavery were false – and probably self-deceived, certainly self-interested – beliefs about the inferior cognitive powers of members of other races. Once these beliefs were overturned, justifications for slavery collapsed without the need for any further theoretical argument.

There is, in contrast, a genuine theoretical dispute about the moral standing of animals. For, as we shall see in Chapters 5 and 7, contractualism entails that such standing should be withheld from animals, while it at the same time accommodates almost all the elements of common-sense moral belief. At no point does this theoretical case rely upon false beliefs about the cognitive powers of animals. Indeed, it is just as much a part of common sense that animals have mental lives in many respects like our own, as it is that their sufferings and interests cannot be counted equally with ours. So, in the case of animals, in contrast with the case of opposition to slavery in the past, utilitarianism is urging a substantial moral change upon us that is insufficiently motivated. Since it will turn out that there is, in fact, a moral theory that would preserve the *status quo* while being equally (at least) as theoretically attractive as utilitarianism, it must be unreasonable for us to accept such a change.

HIGHER AND LOWER PLEASURES

I can think of just one way in which a utilitarian might hope to avoid the consequence that there is no obligation, in an example like that of Saul, the sadist, to opt for the prevention of human suffering above the prevention of animal suffering. This is by appealing to a distinction between higher and lower pleasures, that is in any case sometimes defended by utilitarians. It is sometimes said that there are pleasures, such as those of listening to a Schubert piano sonata, that are higher than others, such as the pleasures of eating or of masturbation.[16] These (broadly intellectual) pleasures are said by some utilitarians to be intrinsically more valuable, counting for more in any calculation of overall utility. This distinction between higher and lower pleasures will loom large in the chapter that follows, but it is worth briefly considering, now, how it might be deployed at this point in the argument.

We might wonder, on the face of it, how the distinction between different orders of pleasure could apply to the example of Saul, the sadist, at all. For in that example no pleasure is in question, only physical pain. And this we are presuming to be the same in both quality and intensity in both human and animal. But this is to forget that one of the characteristic effects of pain, particularly if it is intense, is to interfere with other enjoyments, especially those that are cognitive in nature. Those who doubt this should try making love while suffering from a migraine, or listening to a Schubert sonata with one. It may then be said that while the pain undergone by a human being is intrinsically no more morally significant than the suffering of an animal, the human case is distinctive in that the pain also prevents enjoyment of pleasures that are higher. So the suggestion is that we may explain our intuition in the example of Saul, the sadist, as follows. The human being definitely ought to be the one to be rescued, because if that human were not undergoing torture, then at least some of their time would be occupied with pleasures that are higher than those that would occupy the time of a dog or a monkey if *they* were not being tortured.

As I say, the distinction between higher and lower pleasures will be considered in the next chapter, where I shall argue that it is of doubtful coherence. But it does not, in any case, really get a utilitarian out of the present difficulty, as can easily be seen. For suppose you know that the human who is undergoing torture is a convinced hedonist, of a sort who would in fact devote their entire time to the pursuit of lower pleasures if rescued. Or, if it is thought that experience of torture may be sufficient to cure anyone of hedonism, suppose that the human being in question is mentally retarded, so that they are constitutionally incapable of enjoying any but the lower pleasures. These possibilities make not the slightest difference to my intuition that it would be wrong to do anything other than rescue the human being. In which case, it cannot be the characteristic human capacity for intellectual pleasures that underlies the intuition.

Quality-of-character-utilitarians can perhaps reply to this argument. They can claim that our habit of taking human suffering more seriously than the comparable suffering of an animal has been formed in circumstances in which human suffering normally does (but animal suffering does not) interfere with the pursuit of higher pleasures. Then the intuition that I take so seriously in the case of Saul, the sadist – that it would be wrong to save the dog before the human being – may merely reflect this habitual way of thinking, which itself has a utilitarian justification.

There are two points to be made about this reply. The first is that it is a double edged weapon. For it is plain that most ordinary people do not seriously rate animal suffering at all, in comparison to the sufferings of human beings. A quality-of-character-utilitarian might then be expected to urge, as a corrective to this, that we should try to develop in ourselves a disposition to take animal sufferings *more* seriously than the sufferings of humans. This is on the sound Aristotelian principle that if you are trying to mold a quality of character that is difficult for us to attain, you should aim, initially at least, to exaggerate it – by overshooting the mark, you may hit the target.[17] So the quality of character that is manifested in our judgement that it would be wrong to rescue the dog first is arguably lacking in utilitarian justification in any case, even supposing that the distinction between higher and lower pleasures could be made out. For we ought, on utilitarian grounds, to be trying to become the sort of people who take animal suffering more seriously than we do.

The second point that should be made against the above reply is to note that reflective equilibrium, in its widest sense, must essentially involve comparison *between* moral theories, as well as mutual adjustment of theoretical detail and ordinary belief *within* a given theoretical approach. For I take it that our common-sense intuition in the case of Saul, the sadist, is not simply that it would be wrong to rescue an animal before the human (which might perhaps be explained by appeal to the distinction between higher and lower pleasures), but that it is wrong to weight the suffering of an animal equally with the equal suffering of a human being. So the plausibility of suggesting that our intuition in this case should be rejected needs to be contrasted with the relevant theoretical alternatives. As we shall see in Chapter 7, contractualism can explain all the main elements of common-sense moral belief here without having to give up this intuition. It should, therefore, other things being equal, be preferred – especially given the strength of our feeling on the issue.

SUMMARY

There is an argument for saying that speciesism is just as morally objectionable as racism or sexism. This argument would, if accepted, have important implications for our practices that cause suffering to animals, such as hunting and factory farming, since there are good reasons for believing that higher vertebrates, at least, have interests. But in fact the argument presupposes that the moral standpoint may be equated with that of an impartial sympathetic observer, which is the governing conception of utilitarianism. Moreover, the fact that utilitarianism has such a consequence renders it reflectively unstable, since the conclusion is at odds with apparently fundamental features of our moral thought. Even an appeal to the distinction between higher and lower pleasures cannot really help. The utilitarian approach to animal suffering is therefore inadequate, and should be rejected.

CHAPTER 4

Utilitarianism and the harm of killing

In this chapter I shall conclude my discussion of the implications of utilitarianism for the question of the moral standing of animals, by considering what a utilitarian should say about the value of animal life.

DYING, KILLING, AND HARMING

I argued in Chapter 3 that utilitarians are committed to extending the principle of equal consideration of interests to animals, and that this would then imply that it is morally wrong to cause an animal to suffer, except in unusual circumstances. Some utilitarians, including Singer, have thought that the principle of equal consideration applies to animals very differently when it comes to the question of killing them. Some have argued, indeed, that there is no moral objection to killing an animal, provided that the death is unexpected and painless. We then get a moral position that does not entail moral vegetarianism, while it would rule out hunting and factory farming. Alternatively, some have argued that, while there are moral objections to killing animals, the value of animal life is much lower than that of persons. So although it is wrong to kill an animal for no reason, much less reason is required than is necessary to justify the killing of a person. The main arguments for these views will be considered in later sections. I shall begin by drawing some preliminary distinctions.

It is important to keep three different questions, that are often run together, separate from one another. The first is whether death is harmful to the one who dies, and if so, in what respect it is harmful. There is an ancient puzzle about this. For there is a problem, both about the subject who is harmed by death, and about the time at which the harm occurs. Before a person dies, there is presumably no harm, since death has not yet occurred. But as soon as the moment of death arrives, there is no longer anyone in existence to be harmed. (Since this book is written from a secular perspective, I shall assume throughout that death is the end of existence, for both persons and animals.)[1] Many have, therefore, concluded that death is not, in itself, a harm at all, and that we suffer no evil by dying.

The second question is whether we have reason to be afraid of death. This is easily confused with the first, but is really quite distinct from it. Many who hold that death is not an evil believe that it follows from this that it is irrational to fear death. They argue that those who are afraid of death are mistakenly picturing the time after their death as a sort of positive, but empty, state – the state of existing in utter blankness. Whereas the reality is that those who are dead no longer exist at all. It is then argued that fear of death only arises because we mistakenly confuse the *end* of consciousness with an *empty* consciousness. But this is not so. Even if death is not a harm, it may still be rational to fear it. For our reasons for wanting to go on living are not that we wish to avoid the harm of death, but rather that continued life is a presupposition of most of our projects and desires. That I should not die first is a necessary condition for satisfying almost any desire. (Exceptions would be desires for martyrdom and posthumous fame.) Therefore, in so far as I have desires for the future that require my continued existence, I shall also have reason to fear death. For, in general, we have reason to fear anything that may prevent our desires from being satisfied.

The third question, that is closely related to, but distinct from, the other two, is why it is directly wrong to kill (ignoring side-effects, such as grief caused to loved ones and so on). If death is a harm, then this will receive an answer within utilitarianism – it is because killing causes harm. But even if death is not a harm, it may still be directly wrong to kill, at least from a contractualist perspective. This will be because killing infringes the agent's autonomy – indeed, it is the ultimate infringement of autonomy. Since agents will generally have projects and desires that require their continued existence, they will not wish to be killed. In which case, killing them will infringe their right to pursue their projects without interference. If rational agents have reason to fear death, then it is obvious that rational contractors should agree not to kill one another, except in self-defence.

Our main question in this chapter is whether the direct utilitarian objections to the killing of persons (ignoring side-effects) extend also to the killing of animals. I shall argue that they do. But first we must consider whether death is a harm, and if so, in what respect.

THE HARM OF DEATH

The position of those who believe that death is not a harm may be summed up in the old adage 'What you don't know can't hurt you'. On this view, since those who have died are no longer in existence to feel any deprivation, no harm has resulted to them from their deaths. The old adage is not strictly true, however. Something can harm me if it prevents me from enjoying things that I would otherwise have enjoyed, even if I never know and never feel the lack. Suppose that a rich uncle of whom I have never heard dies, leaving me millions in his will. But I never learn that this has happened, because a clever lawyer manages to defraud me of my inheritance. Here I may rightly be said to have been harmed by the lawyer's action, even though I never feel the lack of the money. For there are many satisfactions that I would have enjoyed had the lawyer not interfered. Preventing someone's satisfaction is just as much a way of harming them as causing them dissatisfaction.

In the light of this, it is obvious that there is one respect in which death is, normally, a harm to the one who dies. (Of course there are circumstances in which life is so awful that continued existence is no blessing – in which the person would be, as we say, better off dead. Recall the example of Anthony, the author, from Chapter 1.) For it will generally be true that if the individual had not died, then they would have continued to enjoy a satisfying existence. Death is then a harm, not because it causes us positive deprivation – not because it causes us felt dissatisfaction – but because it prevents us from enjoying satisfactions that we would otherwise have had. Death is a harm, not because of what it is, but for what it does – it cuts off future worthwhile existence.

Some have argued that there is quite another sense in which death is a harm to the one who dies, namely, that it causes many of that person's desires to be *objectively* dissatisfied.[2] But this will take some explaining. We first of all need to distinguish between objective and subjective satisfactions of desire. A desire is objectively satisfied if the event desired does in fact take place, whether the person knows of it or not. A desire is subjectively satisfied, in contrast, if the person comes to believe that the event desired has taken place, whether it really has or not. Suppose that I want the Washington Redskins to win the Superbowl, for example. Then imagine two scenarios. In the first, the Redskins really do win, but, as a result of some sort of misinformation, I come to believe that they have not. Then my desire is objectively, but not subjectively, satisfied. In the second scenario, the Redskins fail to win, but I somehow come to believe that they have. Then my desire has been subjectively, but not objectively, satisfied.

It might be claimed, against this distinction, that every desire aims at its own subjective satisfaction – in which case it is impossible for a desire to be objectively satisfied without being subjectively satisfied. So it might be said that when I want the Redskins to win the Superbowl, what I really want is the felt satisfaction of learning that they win. But this is plainly false, for two reasons. First, when I am pleased that the Redskins have won, I am pleased *because* I have got what I wanted. The pleasure is a result of my desire being satisfied, not what the desire was really a desire for. Felt satisfaction is a normal concomitant of the knowledge that a desire has been objectively satisfied, rather than being what every desire really aims at. The truth is certainly not that I wanted the Redskins to win because I guessed that their winning would please me! Second, many of our desires in any case aim at things that we know we shall never see happen. For example, many of us have desires for things about which we are quite clear-headed that they will only be realised after our deaths, such as the desire that our grand-children should live to a happy old age. Plainly we are not in this case wanting to *see* our grand-children live to a happy old age (though we may have that – impossible – desire as well).

With the distinction between objective and subjective satis-factions of desire in place, Nagel's thesis can now be stated. It is that both objective and subjective frustrations of desire are a species of harm. Then death is a harm to the one who dies because all of that person's desires for the future that involve their own continued existence are thereby objectively frustrated. For example, if I want to be rich and want to be famous, but die before I can become either, then those desires will have been objectively frustrated. Of course, I will not *feel* any dissat-isfaction, since I shall no longer exist. But it will be true that the things I wanted did not in fact take place, because death prevented them from happening. In which case death has harmed me, if objective frustrations of desire count as harms.

Is Nagel correct to claim, however, that objectively frustrated desires are a species of harm? The question is an important one for us, on the assumption that animals have many fewer, if any, desires for the future (an assumption we shall examine in Chapter 6). For then death will be much less of a harm for them, if a large part of the harm of death for humans consists in the objective frustration of our forward-looking, long-term, desires.

In order to test Nagel's thesis, let us consider an example in some detail. Suppose that Kurt is married to Philippa, and wants very much that Philippa should be faithful to him. Philippa, however, has other ideas, and carries on a love affair with another man without Kurt discovering. Suppose that nothing in Philippa's relationship with Kurt ever suffers as a result – so far as Kurt is concerned, things are just as they would have been if Philippa had in fact been faithful to him throughout. Is Kurt harmed by Philippa's infidelity, merely because his desire that she should be faithful to him is objectively frustrated, and despite the fact it is subjectively satisfied? I do not believe that he is.

I admit to feeling a certain pull in the contrary direction. But I think that this can be explained. For we can distinguish at least two senses in which everyone, including utilitarians, might agree that what Philippa does is bad (quite apart from any question of breach of contract), but which neither of them amount to any misfortune for Kurt. First, we might allow that what Philippa *does* is bad, in the sense that she has taken a real risk of harming Kurt. For no matter how careful she may be, there is always a chance that Kurt will find out. Second, there is a sense in which it is bad for someone to be exposed to risk. Something bad has surely happened to an atomic power worker who becomes contaminated by radiation, for example, because of the risk that this will cause serious disease to develop in later life. But consider the situation after the fact. If the power worker lives to a ripe old age and dies of a heart attack, then no harm was in fact done by the exposure to radiation. Similarly, imagine yourself reviewing Kurt's life shortly after his eventual death. He remained happily married to Philippa throughout and never, in fact, discovered her infidelity. Then surely he was not harmed either. Although something he wanted not to happen did in fact happen, he was not harmed by it. This is because he never knew of it, and because (in the light of our earlier discussion of the fraudulent lawyer) it did not prevent him from enjoying satisfactions that he would otherwise have enjoyed.

For some people, the intuition that Kurt is harmed by Philippa's action may survive the points made above. As someone might put it: 'The harm done to Kurt is that his desire was for the real thing and what he got was fraudulent.'[3] But I think that this intuition derives from a wholly different perspective on ethics (namely, contractualism), and that there is no way in which it can be available to a utilitarian. I shall explain this briefly now, returning to the point, from a slightly different angle, in a later section.

It is true, of course, that what people generally *want* is the real thing, not a plausible substitute. (When Kurt wants Philippa to be faithful to him he wants just that – that she should be faithful – not that he should continue to believe that she has been faithful.) For this reason rational contractors cannot agree to principles that would prohibit them from subjectively frustrating the desires of others in certain circumstances, but allowing them objectively to frustrate those desires, even provided that there is no danger that the person in question should find out. For example, it might plausibly be held that marriage (or at least a certain kind of marriage) gives rise to an obligation to take the important desires and projects of our partners seriously, trying not to frustrate those desires if we can. Now, the important point is that this obligation, viewed from a contractualist perspective, has to be understood as dealing with *objective* satisfactions of desire. Since what we aim at is the real thing, it would be intolerable that we should agree to principles that would give equal credit to plausible substitutes. (This follows, I think, from the contractualist commitment to the ideal of *publicity* in moral principles.) So it may be that Philippa fails in her obligations to Kurt, even supposing that there is no real danger of him finding out.

I thus maintain that the intuition that Kurt has been harmed may derive, in the end, from the fact that wrong has been done him, understood from a contractualist perspective. So this is not a harm that a utilitarian can recognise. To see this clearly, we need an example where the putative harm is caused accidentally (so there is no question of wrong-doing), and where it is clear that there is no danger that objective dissatisfaction should ever become subjective (so there is no harm in the sense of risk, either). To this end, let me introduce the example of Astrid, the astronaut, variants of which will recur at various points through the remainder of this book.

Suppose that Astrid is a very rich woman, who has become tired of life on earth with its squalor and constant violence. Accordingly, she buys herself a space-rocket, and takes off on a trajectory that is set irreversibly to carry her out of our solar system, and forever out of contact with her fellow humans. She does not even carry with her a radio with which she can be contacted. Now suppose that before leaving earth she had erected a statue in memory of her beloved late husband, and one of her most cherished desires is that the statue should outlast her. But within months of her departure the statue is struck by lightning and destroyed. Is Astrid harmed? It seems to me plain that she is not, since she can never know. Yet her desire has been objectively frustrated. This confirms my suggestion that what really underpins the intuition that harm has been done, in cases such as Kurt's, is that *wrong* has been done, involving either a risk of harm, or an infringement of principles that are only intelligible from a contractualist perspective.

I conclude that death is, indeed, a harm to the one who dies, but solely because death prevents future subjective satisfactions of desire (that is to say, continued worthwhile existence), not because it prevents many of the person's desires for the future from being objectively satisfied. Let me stress again, however, that this thesis need not imply corresponding claims about the reasons we have for fearing death, or about the reasons why killing is wrong. To claim that the harm of death consists in preventing subjective satisfactions of desire certainly does not imply that our only reason for fearing death is to gain those satisfactions. On the contrary, almost any desire, whether it be a desire for a feeling of satisfaction or an objective state of affairs, can give one reason to fear death. Nor does that thesis imply that the only possible direct objection to killing is that it prevents future subjective satisfactions. On the contrary, contractualists, at least, will regard most killings as wrong because they infringe autonomy, quite apart from the harm that they do.

THE WRONGNESS OF KILLING

If the conclusions of the previous section are correct, then it is clear that death is a harm to an animal in exactly the same way that it is a harm to a human being – in both cases death (normally) prevents future enjoyments and satisfactions that would otherwise have occurred. It follows that if killing humans is directly wrong, for a utilitarian, because of the harm that it causes – because it cuts off future worthwhile existence – then on precisely the same grounds it must be directly wrong to kill an animal. Since there can be no reason why an impartial

observer should refuse to recognise the enjoyments of an animal
as having moral standing, it would be mere speciesism to claim
that it is wrong to prevent future enjoyments in the case of a
human being without saying the same for an animal.

This is not yet to say that killing an animal would be *as* wrong
as killing a human being, however. For as we shall see in a later
section, some have claimed that the distinctive enjoyments of
human beings have greater moral worth – are 'higher' – than
those of an animal. In which case, although killing an animal
would normally be directly wrong, there might still be no
question of weighing up animal lives against the life of a human.

Even the conclusion that killing an animal is directly wrong
may depend very much on what specific version of utilitarianism
is endorsed, however. If utility is cashed in terms of happiness or
pleasure, then these are apparently states that animals can
enjoy just as much as we can. And then the fact that killing an
animal would prevent future pleasure will be a reason against it,
just as it is a reason against killing a human. But some
utilitarians, including Singer, think that utility is better cashed
in terms of the fulfilment of preferences.[4] On such an account,
the main reason against killing a human being is that most
humans have a strong preference for going on living. But, it is
claimed, most (perhaps all) animals are incapable of having
such a desire. An animal has preferences for satisfaction as
against suffering, but if animals are incapable of conceptualising
their own future non-existence, then they cannot have a
preference for their own future existence, as against non-
existence. In Chapter 6 I shall consider to what extent these
claims about the cognitive powers of animals are true. For the
moment, let us see what follows on the supposition that they are.

A PREFERENCE-UTILITARIAN APPROACH

How should preference-utilitarianism be understood? In particular, is it objective or subjective satisfactions of preference
that are to enter into calculations of utility? Clearly, I think, the
answer has to be that it is subjective satisfactions that matter, for

at least two reasons. First, notice that if it was objective satisfactions of desire that were the basic utilitarian value, then in calculating utility we should be obliged to give as much weight to the preferences of those long dead as to those of the living. Suppose that all the inhabitants of Franksville in the year 1900, for example, wanted very much that the statue of their beloved founder Frank should stand in the town square for as long as the town lasted. None of those people is now living, and the present inhabitants of Franksville find the statue of Frank ugly, and wish to see it removed. Suppose that in the interim the population of the town has shrunk. Then if it is objective satisfactions that are to count, a preference-utilitarian might have to claim that we are morally obliged to keep the statue where it is, since this is the option that objectively satisfies the most desires. This seems intuitively absurd.

The second reason why preference-utilitarianism has to be understood in terms of subjective rather than objective satisfactions is more deeply theoretical. It is that it is impossible to see why an impartial benevolent observer should give any weight to satisfactions of preference that are merely objective. For why should such an observer count it as a good thing that people get what they want, as such, independently of whether or not they believe that they have got it? It is surely no part of benevolence to do something that satisfies someone's desire in circumstances in which the person will never know what has happened.

To make this point vivid, consider a variant of the example of Astrid, the astronaut. As before, the statue of her late husband is destroyed soon after her departure from earth. I argued previously that this cannot be regarded as harming her. Let us now ask whether, knowing her feeling on the matter, I would act benevolently if I were to arrange for the statue to be rebuilt. It is surely clear that I would not. Although such an action would objectively satisfy Astrid's desire, and although it might serve to express my sense of mourning for her absence, it would not now be of any benefit to her. And benevolence surely has to do with the provision of benefit and the prevention of harm.

I conclude that preference-utilitarianism has to be understood in terms of subjective satisfactions of desire. We need to ask next, just *which* desires are to count. Suppose it is replied first, that only presently existing desires are to be considered. Then the desires of animals – for example, to avoid present suffering – may make it wrong to hunt them or factory farm them. But since animals do not, it is supposed, have desires for their own continued existence, it will not be wrong to bring about their deaths. For the future desires of an animal, that would be involved in its continued worthwhile existence if it were not killed, are not to be counted at all, on the present proposal. Since human beings, in contrast, do generally desire continued existence, we are obliged to respect that desire, and killing will normally be directly wrong in consequence.

Notice that the position we have reached here is in many ways a curious one. For so long as an animal has active preferences – so long as it is hungry, or thirsty, or is wanting to play – then the principle of equal consideration of interests will require that we should, other things being equal, try to satisfy those preferences. If there is nothing better that you can achieve with your time and resources, then a preference-utilitarian will have to claim that you are morally obliged to feed a hungry dog. But as soon as the animal no longer has any active preferences – is sitting contentedly after eating, for example, or has fallen asleep – then you would not be failing to fulfil any of its desires if you killed it. So you are obliged to feed the dog while it is hungry, but as soon as it is satisfied you may kill it. This combination of views seems strange, to say the least.

More importantly, if we are required to restrict attention to presently existing preferences, then we can give no moral weight to preferences that we know will exist in the future. For example, suppose that David is subject to temporary fits of severe depression, during which nothing seems worthwhile. At the moment he is suffering such a depression, and has no desire to go on living – he might kill himself if he could only find the energy. But I know perfectly well that by tomorrow he will be back to normal again. If it were only present desires that counted, for a preference-utilitarian, then it would seem that there is no direct moral objection to my killing David. But this is absurd. The fact that he will again have a strong desire for continued life in the future is surely sufficient to make such an action wrong.

Consider another example to reinforce the point. Adolescents and young adults commonly deny vigorously that they ever wish to have children. Indeed, there is no reason to think that they are insincere. But we know that, for most of them, the issue will strike them very differently in a few years' time. Now other things being equal, a policy of offering free sterilisations to such people would surely be wrong, on the grounds that it prevents them from satisfying their future desire to have children. But if only present desires were to be counted, then there would be no direct moral objection to the policy.

I conclude that a preference-utilitarian should certainly give weight to the subjective satisfaction of both present and future desires. But then utilitarians will again be in the position of having to say that there are essentially the same reasons against killing animals as there are against killing human beings. It may be true that animals do not presently have desires for their own continued existence. But it is also normally true that they will have desires for satisfactions and for avoidance of suffering in the future, provided that they are not killed. And these desires should now be given equal weight with any others. Since you should try to ensure the satisfaction of the animal's future desires, you are therefore normally obliged not to kill it.

A human being will have, in general, many more desires at any given time than will an animal. But this is not to the point. What matters, is the number (and intensity) of the desires that can or will be satisfied. And here there need be no difference between human and animal. So preserving the life of a human being will not necessarily lead to more desire satisfaction than would preserving the life of an animal. This will depend upon the details of the cases. The only difference between killing animals and humans thus far is that by not bringing about the death of a human you will generally satisfy one more desire – namely, the presently existing desire for continued life. But in the case of depressed David there will not even be this difference.

If a preference-utilitarian should give weight to both present and future desires, then is the aim simply to maximise desire satisfaction (whether average or total) overall? This can seem counter-intuitive. For one way to comply with it would be to set about creating in people easily satisfied desires. Now, there may not be anything especially wrong with creating such desires. I do not particularly wish to commit myself to condemning consumer society at this point. But there can surely be no moral obligation to support such a society, merely on the grounds that with more and more desires continually being created in people by advertising, more and more desires are continually being satisfied.

There are difficult issues arising here for preference-utilitarianism. Some have attempted to overcome them by retreating to the notion of a *rational* desire, claiming that only present and future desires that qualify as rational ones are to be given moral weight. (Another issue arising is whether it is only the future desires of actually existing creatures that are to be counted. This comes up especially in connection with population policy.)[5] The notion of a rational desire is notoriously difficult to define. For our purposes it will be enough to distinguish two broad approaches to the problem. On the one hand, we could explain the notion of a rational desire in terms of the modes of desire-formation that are normal for the cognition of the creature involved. This would allow animals, and non-rational agents generally, to have rational desires. But then, on the other hand, we could explain the notion of a rational desire in terms of the sorts of processes of thinking and reasoning that are distinctive of rational agents. Taking this option would exclude the future desires of animals from the moral domain once more.

To take this second option would be blatantly speciesist, however. It is impossible to see any reason why an impartial benevolent observer should discount a particular desire, merely because the creature in question had not subjected it to intellectual scrutiny. It is easy to see why such an observer might discount the present desires of depressed David, or desires produced by advertising, hypnosis, or drug addiction. For these desires have been created and sustained by processes that are disruptive of the normal cognitive lives of the agents involved. But there can be no reason why such an observer, if genuinely impartial, should discount or give less weight to the desires of an animal, merely because that animal had failed to engage in such activities as thinking carefully about alternatives, and checking through the presuppositions of its desire for false beliefs.

I conclude that utilitarians, of whatever variety, are committed to saying that the killing of an animal is almost always directly wrong, just as is the killing of a human. The question now is whether a utilitarian must say that killing an animal is just *as* wrong, provided that the number and intensity of the desires or pleasures involved are roughly proportional.

THE VALUE OF LIFE

In addition to the appeal to preference-utilitarianism criticised above, Singer has quite another argument for saying that killing a rational agent – a person – is worse than killing an animal. It is that the lives of rational agents are intrinsically more valuable than the lives of at least most kinds of animal.[6] Now this is not – and had better not be – an appeal to any form of moral intuitionism, which we considered and rejected in the opening chapter. The idea is not that the greater value of human lives is an objective fact, apprehended by us through a special faculty of moral intuition. Rather, Singer's idea is to deploy a version of the classical utilitarian distinction between higher and lower pleasures, transformed now into a distinction between higher and lower modes of life.

It is worth noting that Regan, too, feels obliged to deploy a variant of this distinction, although he is by no means a utilitarian. For he wishes to explain our intuition that, in a case where four men and a dog are adrift on a life-raft that can only safely support four creatures, it is right that the dog should be the one to be thrown off.[7] Regan thinks that the basis for our intuition is that the distinctive enjoyments of a dog have less intrinsic value than those of human beings. Since Regan is not a utilitarian, this is presumably supposed to be one of those objective facts about the world that we are somehow – and mysteriously – to apprehend through the procedure of reflective equilibrium.

The criterion for a pleasure, or a mode of living, being higher, for a utilitarian, is that anyone who has had experience of both would prefer it. Now, we have all had experience of animal pleasures – of a full stomach and a doze in the sun, for example. Yet no one would seriously wish for a life that contained only such pleasures, without the distinctively intellectual enjoyments of reading a novel, listening to music, or engaging in animated conversation with a friend. So it appears to follow that a mode of life that is distinctively human is more valuable than the life of an animal. As Mill famously maintained, it is better to be Socrates dissatisfied than a pig satisfied.

It is easy to see the rationale, for utilitarians, of the distinction between higher and lower pleasures in simple cases. For it provides them with a way of ranking pleasures, in terms other than intensity and duration, that all should rationally agree to. For example, suppose that everyone who has had experience of both, prefers the taste of pineapple to the taste of dry bread. This gives us reason to think that the same would hold even of those who have never tasted pineapple, were they to do so. Suppose Poppy is such a person. Then knowing these facts, she ought rationally to agree that, other things being equal, it is more important that someone should have the pleasure of eating a pineapple than that she herself should have the pleasure of eating dry bread. For she should acknowledge that she, too, were she to experience it, would rank the former pleasure higher.

Problems begin to arise, however, in cases where the character of the subject must undergo substantial change in order to appreciate the new range of pleasures. For this may involve a corresponding inability to appreciate previous enjoyments. For example, many years of disciplined study may be required to appreciate certain intellectual pleasures, such as the pursuit of philosophy or of higher mathematics. But then it may be that the changes of character necessary to appreciate these pleasures unfit one for full enjoyment of singing, dancing, and spontaneity. In which case, the person who has had experience of both sorts of pleasure (that is, the intellectual) is no longer a competent judge of their relative values.

These problems become even more acute when we are trying to compare modes of life across different species. How are we, fairly and realistically, to compare the life of a horse with the life of a human being, given the vast changes in cognitive powers and dispositions that would be necessary to move from the one to the other? Singer attempts to circumvent this problem through the use of an imaginary device.[8] He asks us to imagine a creature with the power to transform itself into each mode of life in turn – living first as a horse, then as a human, and then in some mode different from either, but retaining an exact memory of what each of the first two ways of living was like. Is it not plausible, he asks, that such a creature would judge the life of the human to be more valuable than the life of the horse?

Singer has clearly biased the issue here, however. For note that the creature in question is supposed to have articulate memories of its previous existences, and is supposed to be able to entertain sophisticated judgements about the relative values of those existences. In these respects the mode of existence of that creature is much closer to ours than to that of the horse. Small wonder, then, that such a creature should prefer the life of a human, since it might be expected to judge the life of the horse to be dull and unvaried by comparison. Yet these are, of course, distinctively *human* values, reflecting our relative cognitive complexity and sophistication.

What we have to do is, in fact, well nigh impossible. We have to imagine an impartial benevolent observer – a Martian, perhaps – with interests and mode of cognition no more similar to ours than to those of the horse, who nevertheless has full inside knowledge of what our respective modes of existence are like. In so far as I am able to form any conception of such an observer, I can see no reason why they should judge our human existence to be more valuable than that of the horse. I conclude that while the distinction between higher and lower pleasures may be intelligible and useful for a utilitarian in connection with simple cases, where it is merely lack of experience that prevents a direct comparison, that distinction is useless in attempting to rank pleasures and modes of life across species, with their differing modes of cognition.

THE ELECTRODE WORKERS

I have been arguing that there is no principled way in which utilitarians can show a human life to be more valuable than the life of an animal. It has to be admitted, however, that there is a powerful intuitive appeal behind the sorts of common-sense beliefs that utilitarians try to capture by means of the distinction between higher and lower pleasures. What I shall maintain in this section is that this appeal is only really explicable from the standpoint of contractualism – thus driving one more nail into the coffin of the utilitarian approach to the animals issue.

Consider the following imaginary example, which is grounded in the well-known fact that the brains of many mammals, including rats and monkeys, contain a so-called 'pleasure centre'. If an electrode is inserted into this centre, then the animal in question will engage in an arbitrary activity – such as pressing a bar – for hours on end, in order to have its pleasure centre stimulated. Now imagine that such a centre were discovered in human beings. Suppose also, that some enterprising employers begin to offer implants to their manual workers, in such a way that those workers will have their pleasure centres stimulated every time they make one of the movements required for their work – say, pulling a lever. Those who accept the offer soon come to live for their work and the attendant pleasure it provides. They gladly work a sixteen-hour day, eat on the job, and return home at night only to sleep. They say they cannot understand, now, how anyone else can choose to live differently. Yet there is, surely, a powerful common-sense intuition that their mode of life is impoverished, and that it might be morally wrong to opt for an implant-life, say, by bringing one's child into the factory to be wired up.

It is easy to understand how we, now, would have very good reason not to opt for an implant-life. For all of our current desires, interests, and projects would be lost sight of in such a life. We therefore have almost as much reason to fear an implant as we have to fear death – everything we presently care about would be lost. But at the same time we must recognise that someone who is already an electrode worker has just as much reason to fear the removal of their electrode. For in their case, too, the result would be the loss of everything that they presently care about, in exchange for a set of interests and concerns that they do not currently share. So there is nothing in this that can justify the claim that the one mode of life has, in itself, a greater moral value than the other. (Of course there are all sorts of secondary ways in which those who are not electrode workers may be more useful to other people.) Nor can a utilitarian provide a justification for such a claim through the distinction between higher and lower pleasures. For the positions of each of the two groups with respect to the other will be symmetrical – I presume that each would prefer their present mode of existence to their past one.

Yet the intuition that there is a moral difference here is surely very powerful. Suppose, for example, that the implant has to be made, and wired up regularly, quite early in life in order to be fully successful. You are now considering whether to have an implant made in the brain of your ten-year old son, Imri. If you do so, you know that you will be more or less ensuring his future happiness! For he will then have just one overwhelming desire, that will be easily, and almost continually, satisfied. Yet it would be very wrong of you, surely, to commit Imri to such a future. For in the circumstances you know that, once wired up, he will never want to change – indeed, he will never again have a serious desire for anything else.

This intuition is only really explicable from a contractualist perspective, given that we believe that the electrode workers fail to retain the capacity for planning and choosing that is distinctive of rational agency. (For extended discussion of what is involved in the notion of a rational agent, see Chapter 6.) I think we are inclined to maintain that the desire for pleasure so dominates their cognition as to leave no place for the exercise of genuine autonomy. In fact, their situation is exactly like that of a willing drug addict, only without the debilitating effects of drug addiction. The electrode workers retain the *potential* for rational agency, of course, since if unplugged they would soon return to normal. Indeed, there is a real sense in which they continue to have the *capacity* for it, too, since their minds presumably retain the cognitive structures necessary for autonomous action. It is merely that their implant prevents them from exercising this capacity – just as cotton wool packaging can prevent a brittle glass from exercising its capacity to be broken. (Seen in this light, there would then be a powerful case for rescuing the electrode workers from their plight, overriding their own vigorous resistance – though this is not the point I particularly wish to focus on.)

What this then means is that it will be *us*, rather than the electrode workers, who get to frame the terms of the moral contract. For moral rules, within contractualism, are created by rational, choosing, autonomous agents. To put the point slightly differently, the electrode workers cannot reasonably reject any proposed system of rules, since their situation is such that they are no longer capable of exercising their capacity for rational decision. So they can be allowed to have no objection to any rules that might be proposed, including those that would prevent Imri from becoming an implant boy. What would be more natural, then, than that we should decide to outlaw practices that undermine the exercise of genuine autonomy, as would becoming an electrode worker in childhood? For our status as autonomous agents is presupposed in almost everything that we care about. What therefore emerges, is that a contractualist should claim, in a way that a utilitarian cannot, that it would be directly wrong to take Imri into the factory to be wired up – which is just what our common-sense intuition tells us.

LIFE AS A JOURNEY

Singer has, more recently, made yet another attempt to ground his view that the lives of rational agents are more valuable than the lives of animals, while retaining his utilitarian perspective. He argues that a human life may usefully be conceived of as a journey.⁹ If I am travelling on a journey, but am forced to abandon it, my disappointment will generally be in proportion to my nearness to the goal, and to the amount of effort that has gone in to the travelling, which now turns out to have been wasted. So, too, in life, Singer thinks. Much of early life is mere preparation for what follows, and many of us have long-term projects that give shape to, and help to make sense of, our lives. It is then less tragic if death should occur early in childhood, when the journey has barely begun, or late in life, when most goals have been attained, and most projects completed. There is also held to be less direct moral objection to killing human beings at these stages in their lives.

Most importantly for our purposes, Singer argues that the point at which the journey of life begins, from the perspective of those who travel, is the point at which they first begin to conceive of themselves as having a future and a past, and to think of some of their current activities as preparatory for the future. For suppose that this were so, and that most animals lack such a conception of themselves altogether (an assumption we shall examine in Chapter 6). Then such an animal will never have embarked on the journey, and death, for them, will be no tragedy, since it does not interrupt any journey. Nor will there be any direct moral objection to killing such a creature.

I can see no theoretical rationale for these views, however. Why should an impartial benevolent observer give less weight to (or discount altogether) the interests of someone who is standing still, as against someone who has embarked on a journey? Those who stay at home have desires, purposes, and feelings no less than those who go abroad. What may be true is that an observer who is comparing two travellers will count as more serious an interruption in the journey of the one who is closest to completion, other things being equal. For, having invested more, that person will have more to lose. But this provides no ground for thinking that an impartial observer will only consider the interests of those who travel (that is, of those who have long-term plans and projects). In which case, we have been given no reason why a utilitarian should maintain that the death of an animal, or a baby, is less serious than the death of a rational agent. On the contrary, the fact that death prevents future satisfaction of desires in all these cases provides the same (and the only) direct utilitarian rationale against killing.

It is true that the judgements Singer seeks to explain through the metaphor of a journey have, for many people, an intuitive appeal. Many do feel that the death of a baby, or an old person, is less of a tragedy, from the perspective of the one who dies, than the death of someone in the prime of life. But I think these intuitions are not utilitarian ones, and certainly provide no basis on which a utilitarian can claim that the death of an animal is less morally significant than the death of a rational agent. Let me explain.

Take the case of babies first. Anyone who has contractualist sympathies might be expected to share the thought that the death of a baby, by accident or from natural causes, is less of a tragedy, from the perspective of the baby, than the death of a normal adult. For such people may be expected to value rational agency above all else, and the baby is presumably not, as yet, a rational agent. (It is arguable, indeed, that all rational agents will value the possession of rational agency highly, quite apart from whatever moral views they may hold.)[10] But it should be emphasised that this is not to claim that a contractualist will count the *killing* of a baby to be less serious than the killing of an adult, as we shall see in the next chapter. Nor is there any way in which utilitarians can motivate the claim that the death of a baby is less morally serious, unless they retreat to a form of indefensible intuitionism, claiming that it is an objective fact about the world that those who have a conception of their past and future are more valuable than those who do not. For, as we have seen, there is no reason why an impartial observer should discount the present and future desires of the baby, merely because they are not yet linked together by any overall life-plan.

Now consider the case of the very old. Again, many share the feeling that the death of such a person is less of a tragedy than the death of a young adult. But these judgements serve mainly to express a comparison with reasonable expectations, made to console the living (like saying 'He had a good innings') – which need not be a point of view shared by the one who has died. It is true that some old people may gradually wind down their activities and projects as they near the term of their expected span. And in some such cases it may rightly be said that the person had little more to live for by the time of their death. But others keep going as they have always done, as if death were only for others. (Interestingly, members of the latter group tend also to live longer.) There is nothing here to support the view that life, as such, may be thought of as a journey – only that some people may conceive of their lives in some such terms.

REFLECTIVE DISEQUILIBRIUM

I conclude that utilitarians are committed to the view that there is the same sort of direct moral objection to killing animals as there is to killing humans. For there are essentially the same utilitarian reasons against such killings in both cases – that killing would prevent future enjoyment, and that not killing is necessary if the organism is to have its future preferences fulfilled. Moreover, there is no coherent way for a utilitarian to claim that the life of a human being has, in itself, greater moral value than the life of an animal, without degenerating into moral intuitionism. The only valid utilitarian reasons remaining, for why it will generally be worse to kill a human being than to kill an animal, are extrinsic ones. These are, first, that human beings tend to live longer than most animals, so a greater extent of life will generally be cut off by death. And second, that the death of a human being will generally cause much suffering to friends and relatives, in a way that the death of an animal will rarely cause suffering to other animals.

Can such a position be acceptable under reflective equilibrium? I believe not. Consider the following development of the example of Kenneth, the kennel owner, first presented in Chapter 1. You arrive at a fire in his dogs' home to find Kenneth unconscious on the floor, while the dogs are still locked in their cages. You judge that you have just enough time either to drag Kenneth to safety or to unlock the cages, but not both. Suppose you also know that Kenneth is quite old, and is something of a recluse who lives entirely for his work, without anyone to care for him. In these circumstances a utilitarian is clearly committed to the view that you should opt to rescue the dogs. For this is obviously the way to ensure the greatest future pleasure, and/or the greatest future desire satisfaction. Utilitarians cannot avoid this conclusion by discounting the interests of the dogs altogether, without engaging in a form of speciesism which must be unacceptable from their own perspective.

This conclusion is morally outrageous, however, as are its further consequences. Once it is accepted that the killing of an animal is just as morally serious, in general, as the killing of a human being, then those practices that involve the regular slaughter of animals, such as farming and some forms of animal experimentation, will seem to fall within the same moral category as the Nazi holocaust. And then any form of opposition to such practices, of whatever degree of violence, will seem eminently justified. In fact, those animals rights activists who pursue the methods of terrorism – planting bombs and poisoning baby-foods – are only following utilitarianism through to its logical, but morally abhorrent, conclusion.

Our common-sense, pre-theoretical, view is that it would be very wrong to place the lives of many dogs over the life of a single (albeit old and friendless) human. This belief is probably too firmly held, in the case of most of us, to be shaken by theoretical argument. (Recall from Chapter 1, indeed, that it is a belief shared even by those philosophers who have been most vociferous in defence of animals, namely Regan and Singer.) Moreover, since this common-sense belief will prove to be retained under contractualism (as we shall see in later chapters) but is lost under utilitarianism, and since contractualism is in other respects just as, if not more, theoretically satisfying than utilitarianism, the correct response is to reject utilitarianism altogether. At any rate, the utilitarian approach to animal lives seems just as unacceptable as we found the utilitarian approach to animal suffering to be in the last chapter.

SUMMARY

Death is a harm to the one who dies only in so far as it prevents future worthwhile existence. Yet our reason for fearing death is that continued life will be presupposed by almost all of our desires. From a utilitarian perspective there is essentially the same direct moral objection to killing an animal as there is to killing a human – namely, that the death prevents future enjoyments, and that not being killed is a necessary condition for the future desires of the creature to be satisfied. From the same perspective there is no reason to count the life of an animal as less valuable than the life of a rational agent. I have argued that these consequences are too extreme to be believed.

CHAPTER 5

Contractualism and animals

In this chapter I shall consider what a contractualist should say about the moral standing of animals. Throughout, I shall make the simplifying assumption that no animals should be counted as rational agents, in the sense that is central to contractualism. The extent to which this assumption is true will be examined in the chapter that follows.

RAWLS'S CONTRACTUALISM AND ANIMALS

According to Rawls, we are to think of morality as the set of rules that would be agreed upon by rational agents choosing from behind a veil of ignorance. While these agents are supposed to have knowledge of all general truths of psychology, economics, and so on, they are to be ignorant of their own particular qualities (their intelligence, physical strength, projects, and desires), as well as the position they will occupy in the resulting society. Their choice of moral principles is to be made in the light of broadly self-interested desires (such as those for happiness, freedom, and power) that the agents know they will possess whatever particular desires and interests they subsequently come to have.

Morality is here pictured as a system of rules to govern the interaction of rational agents within society. It therefore seems inevitable, on the face of it, that only rational agents will be assigned direct rights on this approach. Since it is rational agents who are to choose the system of rules, and choose self-interestedly, it is only rational agents who will have their position protected under the rules. There seems no reason why rights should be assigned to non-rational agents. Animals will, therefore, have no moral standing under Rawlsian contractualism, in so far as they do not count as rational agents.

It might be suggested that there is, after all, a way in which rights can come to be assigned to animals under contractualism. This is by some of the agents behind the veil of ignorance being detailed to speak on behalf of non-rational agents, their task being to represent the interests of animals in the formulation of the basic contract. Compare the way in which a lawyer may represent the interests of a pet dog in a court of law, in a dispute over the deceased owner's will. The idea is that behind the veil of ignorance, as in the law court, someone may be detailed to speak for those who are incapable of speaking for themselves.

Notice, however, that even if this extension of Rawls's theory were acceptable, it would still not yield anything like the common-sense view of animals. On the contrary, it would lead to animals being accorded *equal* rights with human beings, consistent with their different needs and capacities. (Thus one would not expect that animals could have an equal right to own property, since they are incapable of buying and selling. But they could have an equal right to life, and an equal right not to be made to suffer.) There is no reason why the animal representatives behind the veil of ignorance should settle for anything less. For remember that the people in this position are not supposed to have, as yet, any moral beliefs. So the representatives of animal interests cannot accept as a reason for according animals unequal status, that animals have lower moral importance than human beings. But the idea that animals should be given equal standing with ourselves is a good deal more extreme than we should be prepared to accept, as we have seen over the last two chapters.

Another problem with the above suggestion is this. Once it is allowed that animals may have representatives to speak on their behalf behind the veil of ignorance, there seems no good theoretical reason why other sorts of thing should not have representatives also. Why should there not be people detailed to defend plants and micro-organisms, or indeed mountains and ancient buildings? Moral rights would then become rampant, in a way that would, I think, be acceptable to no one.

The main objection to allowing representatives of animal interests behind the veil of ignorance, however, is that it is arbitrary. It has been done without any independent theoretical rationale, simply to secure the desired result – that animals should have moral standing. Now it might seem that this charge is unfair. For as Rawls stresses, the business of theory-construction in morality is, at least partly, a matter of seeking reflective equilibrium. Although moral beliefs should not be directly mentioned within our theory, it is a constraint on a theory being acceptable that it should deliver a good many, at least, of our firmly held moral convictions. And we do have moral convictions about the appropriate treatment of animals. So it might be said that allowing representatives to speak on behalf of animals behind the veil of ignorance is just the sort of theoretical alteration that we ought to have expected to make all along.

While I have endorsed the method of reflective equilibrium in ethics, I do not think that it can be successful in defending the current proposal. One reason for this is that the proposal does not, in any case, deliver the common-sense view of animals, as I pointed out above. But a more important reason is as follows. As initially presented, the idea of choice of moral principles from a position of ignorance constituted a coherent vision of the nature and source of morality. Moral rules were seen as those that rational agents would agree on to govern their conduct with respect to one another, if they employed only general rational considerations in their choice, not allowing themselves to be influenced by facts about their own particular interests or position within society. But if some of these agents are detailed to represent the interests of animals in the selection of moral rules, this coherence vanishes. It is then no longer clear what morality *is*. Indeed, it appears that we would have to say – circularly – that morality is the set of rules that would be agreed upon by rational agents who already had a prior belief in the moral standing of animals.

Regan has mounted an argument designed to show that contractualism cannot coherently withhold moral standing from animals, without also withholding it from those human beings who are not rational agents, such as severe mental defectives or senile old people.[1] I shall defer considering the latter part of this charge until later sections, where it will turn out that Regan seriously underestimates the resources available to contractualists, through which they can explain how all human beings should be accorded the same basic moral rights, whatever their mental capacities. Here I shall consider Regan's argument that Rawlsian contractualism is theoretically arbitrary to the extent that it denies moral standing to animals.

Regan claims that if agents behind the veil of ignorance are to be ignorant of such fundamental matters as their qualities of character, life-plans, and position within society, then there is no good reason why they should not also be ignorant of their species. But if the agents were to be ignorant of the species into which they would subsequently be incarnated, when selecting basic moral principles, then, plainly, they would choose rules protecting the interests of members of all species equally. So Rawls has simply begged the question against the moral standing of animals in the manner in which he sets up the apparatus of the veil of ignorance. Had he arranged the details of that device slightly differently, then animals would have been accorded the same basic rights as human beings within contractualism.

Now, I do not wish to suggest that there is anything sacrosanct about the way in which Rawls characterises the details of the veil of ignorance. (On the contrary, it is plain that a simple extension of his ideas would deliver a strong environmental ethic that would at the same time be theoretically motivated. We need only suppose that the agents behind the veil of ignorance should have a desire to inhabit a healthy environment, besides desires for the primary goods of happiness, freedom, and power. This would immediately lead to agreement on principles that protect the environment. Yet it would have a theoretical rationale, in that rational agents may surely know that, whatever else they may want, they will also wish to live in an environment that is healthy and pleasant.) Nevertheless, I do not think that the extension suggested by Regan – that agents behind the veil of ignorance should be ignorant of their species – is a coherent one, as I shall now try to explain.

An initial problem is that Regan misinterprets Rawls. He takes him to believe that the veil of ignorance is a genuine metaphysical possibility – that rational agents might really exist in ignorance of their character, desires, strength, sex, and social position, perhaps as disembodied souls – whereas it is, for Rawls, only a device for bracketing unwanted knowledge, whose point is to ensure that we should not, in the construction of moral principles, appeal to knowledge that might undermine the reasonableness of the result.[2] This does not yet dispose of Regan's argument, however. For it is presumably possible that rational agents should bracket their status as rational agents, even in the very process of rationally constructing a system of rules. If they can forbear from making use of their knowledge of their sex or social status, then presumably they can just as well forbear from making use of their knowledge of their species or, indeed, of the fact that they are rational agents.

The real line of reply to Regan is that his suggestion would destroy the theoretical coherence of Rawlsian contractualism. As Rawls has it, morality is, in fact, a human construction (in the absence, that is, of any other known species of rational agent – a point I shall return to in the next chapter). Morality is viewed as constructed *by* human beings, in order to facilitate interactions *between* human beings, and to make possible a life of co-operative community. This is, indeed, an essential part of the governing conception of contractualism. It is crucial to its explanation of how moral notions can arise, avoiding the excesses of intuitionism and strong objectivism. It is also presupposed by contractualist accounts of the source of moral motivation, whether in the Rawlsian version (to make peaceful human community possible in conditions of modernity) or in my own, where the basic contractualist concept (as well as the desire to comply with it) is held to be innate, selected for in evolution because of its value in promoting the survival of our species. To suggest, now, that contractualism should be so construed as to accord equal moral standing to animals would be to lose our grip on where moral notions are supposed to come from, or why we should care about them when they arrive.

It may be objected that this line of reply to Regan implausibly reduces morality to anthropology. But in fact it does no such thing. My claim is not that moral statements are really disguised claims about the conditions for the survival of the species. On the contrary, they are about what rational agents should reasonably accept who share the aim of reaching free and unforced agreement. My claim is only that we have this concept of morality innately, and have an innate desire to justify our actions in terms that others may freely accept, because doing so has promoted the survival of our species in the past. But if the contractualist concept expresses what morality *is*, for us, then there is no moral standpoint from which it can be criticised, or from which it can be argued that we are morally required to extend that concept so as to accord equal moral standing to animals.

I conclude, therefore, that Regan is mistaken. Rawls is by no means arbitrary in allowing agents behind the veil of ignorance to have knowledge of their species and their status as rational agents. On the contrary, this is crucial to ensure the plausibility of the contractualist governing conception of the source of moral notions and moral motivation.

SCANLON'S CONTRACTUALISM AND ANIMALS

The points made above in reply to Regan strongly suggest that the exclusion of moral standing from animals is entailed by contractualism as such, rather than by any mere quirk of Rawls's presentation. As a cross-check on this, let us briefly consider how animals would fare under Scanlon's version of contractualism, in which the agents concerned are supposed to be real ones, possessing full knowledge of their own idiosyncratic desires and qualities, and their position within the current structure of society. Recall that on Scanlon's account, moral rules are those that no one could reasonably reject as a basis for free, unforced, agreement, who shares the aim of reaching such agreement. The only idealisations made are that choices and objections will always be rational, and that all concerned will share the aim of reaching such an agreement.

We still have here a coherent vision of the nature of morality – indeed, essentially the same vision as is presented in Rawls's contractualism. Since Scanlon's model deals with real agents, however, with their individual desires and concerns, and since many real agents care deeply about the welfare of some or all animals, there is then a genuine question as to whether such people might not reasonably reject rules that give no weight to the interests of animals. It may be that animals will turn out to have moral standing in this version of contractualism, because many of the contracting parties care deeply about them.

What we need to know is: what counts as a reasonable basis on which to reject a proposed rule? It seems clear at least that it will not be reasonable for someone to reject a rule, if others would have an equal basis on which to reject *any* proposed rule. For in that case we should not be able to satisfy our shared aim of reaching free and unforced general agreement. It cannot be reasonable, therefore, to reject a rule merely because it conflicts with some interest or concern of mine. For every rule (except the entirely trivial) will conflict with someone's concerns. Perhaps I care deeply about the welfare of animals. But then others care deeply about standards of dress and appearance, modes of sexual activity, and the worship of their god. If I can reasonably reject rules that accord no weight to the interests of animals, then others can equally reasonably reject rules that allow us to dress and make love as we wish, and to worship or not worship as we please. Even rules against killing might be equally reasonably rejected by some people, since they may want very much to kill those who stand in their way.

What *can* be reasonably rejected are rules that accord no weight to my interests in general, or rules that allow my privacy to be invaded, or my projects to be interfered with, at the whim of other people. For, since I know that others will similarly have reason to reject a rule that allows me to interfere in their lives, and I desire that we should agree on some rules to govern our conduct, I shall be happy to give up my right to interfere in the lives of others in order to gain an equal protection against interference in my own life. Indeed, it appears that here, as before, the basic principle that we should agree upon is one of respect for the autonomy of rational agents.

I therefore conclude that Scanlon's contractualism, like Rawls's, will fail to give moral standing to animals, in so far as animals do not themselves have the status of rational agents. But let me stress again that this is not to say that a contractualist cannot care very deeply about animals. The point is that not all cares and concerns are moral ones. Just as someone can care deeply about architecture without believing that some buildings have moral standing, or that those buildings have a right to be preserved (not derivative from the fact that people such as themselves care deeply about them); in the same way one can be an animal lover without thinking that animals have rights.

TWO VARIETIES OF INDIRECT SIGNIFICANCE

The claim that animals must lack moral standing under contractualism does not necessarily imply that one can, with impunity, do whatever one wishes with respect to any animal. For they may yet have indirect moral significance. This remains to be investigated. The issue is important because we do need to consider whether contractualism can at least approach our common-sense attitude to animals. If contractualism cannot explain any of our ordinary moral judgements in this domain, then that will count against its acceptability as a moral theory, under reflective equilibrium. Two obvious ways in which contractualism might accord indirect moral significance to animals would be to subsume animals under the rules dealing with private property, or by treating them as a matter of legitimate public interest. Let us consider each of these in turn.

If contractualism would condone a system of property rights, as seems plausible, then it is clear that at least some animals will be protected by those rights. If you have the right against me that I should not, other things being equal, destroy your property, then I am morally obliged not to kill your dog, just as I am obliged not to set light to your car. But notice that it is *your* rights that I would infringe, not the dog's. Indeed, the dog would have no rights, any more than the car does. Notice, moreover, that a great many animals, including those in the wild, will not be protected by property rights, since they have no owners (though some may receive legal protection in national parks or game reserves). More importantly, perhaps, even those animals that have owners will receive no protection against their owners. Since I am within my rights to batter or destroy my car, if I choose to do so, I should also be within my rights to batter or destroy my dog, on this approach. It seems that an appeal to property rights cannot take us very far in attempting to reconcile contractualism with common-sense attitudes.

A more plausible approach would be to appeal to the fact that many people care deeply about animals. For this may then make the manner of our treatment of animals a matter of legitimate public interest. Compare the fact that many people care deeply about architecture and the aesthetics of their environment. This may be sufficient to give rise to a moral duty, on the part of the owners of some attractive ancient building, not to destroy or alter it, except for very powerful reasons (such as that the building has, through previous neglect, become a danger to life). The general point is that one might expect contracting rational agents to reject rules that place no side-constraints on the rights of ownership. Where the objects privately owned are nevertheless a matter of legitimate public enjoyment or interest, it may be reasonable that owners' rights of disposal of their property should be constrained, to some degree.

Similarly, then, in the case of animals. Since many people have concerns for animals, and are deeply distressed at seeing an animal suffer, this may place on us an obligation not to cause suffering to animals, except for powerful reasons. This would not be because needlessly causing such suffering would violate the rights of the animal, any more than someone who defaces a beautiful building violates the rights of the building. On this approach animals, like buildings, would have no direct rights or moral standing. Rather, causing suffering to an animal would violate the right of animal lovers to have their concerns respected and taken seriously.

Such an approach may be able to recover for contractualism a great deal of what common-sense tells us about the moral treatment of animals. In particular, it can explain how it can be true that, while we do have duties towards animals, their lives and interests cannot be weighed against the lives and interests of humans. For the duties in question only arise indirectly, out of respect for those who care about animals. And this duty of respect may surely be overridden where someone's more fundamental interests or very life are threatened. Thus consider, once again, the example of the ancient building. If the building is the owner's only residence, and if structural changes are necessary to make it habitable, then it is surely permissible that it should be altered, overriding the interests of the wider public.

Just how strong would the side-constraints on animal suffering be, on this approach, resulting from the legitimate feelings of animal lovers? Plainly, as we have just seen, they would fail to rule out actions causing suffering to animals that are necessary to subserve some important human concern, such as, arguably, the testing of new medicines upon animals. But more importantly, the constraints would only apply to suffering that occurs in a manner that is unavoidably public. So, in particular, painful methods of factory farming, and the testing of detergents on animals, would not be ruled out, even granting that the purposes subserved by such activities (cheaper meat, and new varieties of shampoo) are trivial. For it seems that one can legitimately reply to those who complain of such activities in exactly the way that one would reply to those who are distressed by unusual sexual practices, for example. One can say: 'If it upsets you, don't think about it.' While granting that an unusual sexual practice (or the suffering of an animal) should not be flaunted in public, because of the offence this may occasion, it seems there can be no objection to it occurring in private. So while the present suggestion concerning the contractualist attitude to animals can accommodate a good deal of common-sense belief, it gives no support to those who are currently campaigning on behalf of factory farmed and laboratory animals.

The present approach does face difficulties, however, quite apart from its consequences for the controversial practices of factory farming and laboratory testing. For there are two important elements of common-sense moral belief that it cannot accommodate. The first is that duties towards animals can arise equally in the private as in the public domain. While the approach can explain why it may be wrong to beat a dog severely in the street, it is not obvious why it should also be wrong to torture a cat in the privacy of your own home. For those people who would be distressed by the cat's suffering, were they to observe it, will in fact remain unaware of it. Yet it may be said that such an action would still, intuitively, be very wrong. Secondly, it is also part of common-sense belief that cruelty to an animal is wrong because of what is done to the animal, not because of any suffering caused to sympathetic human observers, as the present approach would suggest.

There is perhaps more that contractualists can say in their defence along these general lines. For example, since animals, unlike most items of property, are capable of independent motion, there is a greater risk that supposedly private actions may become public. If the cat were to manage to escape from me into the public domain while I am torturing it, then other people may yet become distressed at its condition. Such considerations are plainly pretty weak, however, as the following development of the example of Astrid, the astronaut, will make especially clear.

Recall that Astrid has left earth on a space-rocket, on an irreversible trajectory that will take her out of the solar system and forever out of contact with her fellow human beings. Now in her rocket she carries with her a cat, and a famous work of art of which she is the legitimate owner (the *Mona Lisa*, say). As the years pass she becomes bored with her books and tapes, and seeks alternative entertainment. Then contrast two cases: in the first case she removes the glass cover from the *Mona Lisa* and uses the painting as a dart-board; in the second case she ties the cat to the wall and uses *it* as a dart-board. I think we should feel intuitively that there is a very great difference, morally speaking, between these two cases. This cannot be explained on the hypothesis that our duties towards animals, as towards beautiful objects, arise only out of the likely effect of our actions on the feelings of other people. For both cases are alike in that it can be known that there will be no such effect.

I think I would be prepared to grant that Astrid does nothing wrong in throwing darts at the *Mona Lisa*. I may regret her philistinism, but cannot claim that she violates any rights or omits any moral duties. For it is in any case true that no one else is ever going to see the painting again. (I might say that Astrid had acted wrongly in taking such a great painting with her in the first place, but that is another matter.) In contrast, it is surely wrong of Astrid to throw darts at the cat out of idle amusement, despite the fact that she may be quite certain that no person will ever become distressed at what she has done, since no one will ever know. I therefore conclude that contractualism cannot accommodate all of what common sense tells us about the moral treatment of animals, by trying to give animals an indirect moral significance based upon the fact that many people care deeply about them. We face a choice, at this point, of either giving up contractualist approaches to morality, or giving up some common-sense beliefs.

It might be argued that the conflict with ordinary belief on this matter is not a serious problem for contractualism, since it only really arises in connection with imaginary examples. For in any real case of private cruelty to an animal there will be a danger that the public should become aware of it. But there are two replies to this. The first is that imaginary examples cannot be belittled merely because they are imaginary. When we consider the case of Astrid, the astronaut, we feel very strongly that it would be wrong of her to throw darts at her cat. This attitude has as much right as any other to be considered as part of common sense, even though the example is not real. For the way in which we respond to that example is perfectly real. The second reply is that common sense does not, in any case, merely tell us that cruelty to an animal is wrong. It also tells us that it is wrong because of what is done to the animal, rather than because of the effects on a likely observer. This has not yet been accounted for.

A PROBLEM FOR REFLECTIVE EQUILIBRIUM

As we have just seen, there is a problem for contractualism in attempting to reconcile itself with our common-sense beliefs concerning the appropriate moral treatment of animals. I propose to leave this aside for the moment. I shall return to it in Chapter 7, where I shall show how contractualism can achieve reflective equilibrium on these matters. I shall now pursue a more direct and serious challenge. For contractualism does not just come into apparent conflict with common-sense morality in connection with animals. It also faces difficulties concerning the moral treatment of those human beings who are not, on any account of the matter, rational agents, such as young babies, very senile old people, or severe mental defectives. This is a much more serious difficulty, since the beliefs in question are more centrally embedded within common-sense morality.

If animals are not accorded moral standing under con-tractualism, on the grounds that they are not rational agents, then it would seem that by the same token all those human beings who are not rational agents will also fail to have moral standing bestowed on them. In which case killing a baby or a senile human being would not violate their rights, since they would have no rights. Such killings would at most violate our duty to respect the feelings of those people who care about babies (or that particular baby) or the senile. This is, to say the least, counter-intuitive.

In the case of babies there may be more that a contractualist can say to explain the wrongness of causing them suffering. For such suffering may be expected to have an effect on the rational agents they will one day become. Our actions may thus directly violate the rights of those future persons, and hence be wrong even when done in private so as to cause no distress to others. In the same way, contractualists may be able to explain the wrongness of killing babies, if they are prepared to accept the principle that it is wrong to prevent a rational agent from coming into existence. (What they say about this will clearly have implications for their attitude towards abortion and contraception.) But they cannot similarly explain the wrongness of killing or causing suffering to mental defectives or senile old people, since such human beings no longer have the potential, in general, to become rational agents.

To make the case as strong as possible, consider again the example of Astrid, the astronaut. Suppose that Astrid has taken her grandfather with her, who becomes increasingly senile as the journey progresses. Would it not be very wrong of her to start using *him* as a dart-board to relieve her tedium, or to kill him because the sight of his dribbling offends her? Yet on what grounds can such actions be wrong, if only rational agents have moral standing? For no other person will ever be worried or upset at the suffering or death of her grandfather.

It appears that contractualism faces severe difficulties in accommodating our common-sense attitudes towards those living beings who are not rational agents. Since these attitudes are even more deeply entrenched in connection with non-rational human beings than they are in connection with animals, any attempt to brush common-sense beliefs aside, on the grounds of their conflict with the theory of contractualism, will be correspondingly weaker. For example, no one is going to accept the testing of detergents on the senile, or the hunting of mental defectives for sport. If we cannot find some other way of handling these examples within contractualism, it would appear that the latter is doomed as an acceptable moral theory. I shall now consider a number of different ways in which contractualists might respond.

FAMILY LINES AND THE PROSPECT OF SENILITY

Rawls himself has a way of securing direct moral rights for all human beings. This is by making the agents behind the veil of ignorance choose on behalf, not just of themselves, but of family lines.[3] The main point of this proposal for Rawls is to give the same weight to future generations as to the people of the present in the application of the difference principle – arguing, for example, that it would be wrong of us to exhaust the earth's natural resources. But the proposal is equally serviceable in according rights to babies, the senile, and mental defectives. For it has the effect of securing the same moral rights, not just for all rational agents, but also for all children of rational agents. Then, since every human being – whether baby, senile, or mental defective – is the child of (or, at any rate, is descended from) rational agents, the conclusion will be that all human beings have the same basic moral rights. But since no animals are descended from rational agents, we are supposing, no animals will have direct rights.

The first thing that needs to be asked is whether the position can be properly theoretically motivated. Or is it theoretically arbitrary, like the suggestion discussed earlier, that some people behind the veil of ignorance might be delegated to represent the interests of animals? Remember that those behind the veil of ignorance are to have knowledge of all general facts about the human condition, as well as about human psychology. They will therefore know that it is highly likely that they will have children, and that they will care very deeply what happens to those children. It then appears entirely reasonable that they should insist on direct rights for all children of rational agents (and hence for all human beings). Rather than being arbitrary, the present proposal flows directly from Rawls's character-isation of the veil of ignorance.

This is one of those places where the artificiality of Rawls's construction may matter, however. For it is not nearly so obvious that the above argument can survive translation into other varieties of contractualism. Consider Scanlon's version, for example. Many real agents know that they will never have children. Others may know that their parents have died before becoming senile. Such persons might, it seems, reasonably reject rules according direct moral rights to babies, mental defectives, or the senile. This is in just the same way that those who know that they are indifferent to art may reasonably reject the proposal put forward by the majority of people who are art-lovers, that works of art should be accorded direct moral rights. If we are to find convincing contractualist arguments for according moral standing to all human beings, it seems we should look elsewhere.

A different suggestion is as follows. As a rational agent I know that it is likely that I shall, one day, slide gradually into a condition of senility. I also know that it is possible for an accident to reduce me to the level of a severe mental defective, or a baby. But, it is claimed, I would surely wish to preserve for myself the same basic moral rights and protections in those circumstances as I now enjoy. If I were actually in a state of senility, of course, I should be in no position rationally to reject a system of rules withholding moral rights from the senile. But I may now rationally reject such rules, on the grounds that they conflict with what I want for myself were I to become senile, and since I can see that all have as much reason as myself to reject such rules.

If the argument above were successful, then we might be able to move on to grant moral standing to all human beings, irrespective of their cognitive powers. For, given that moral standing is to be accorded to those who *become* senile, or severely subnormal as a result of an accident, it would surely be intolerable that moral standing should be withheld from those who are *born* so. And then if moral standing is granted to those who, as adults, are congenitally severely subnormal, it would seem that there can be no rational basis for withholding it from young babies, who may enjoy similar levels of cognitive activity.

There are two reasons why this attempt to extend the same basic rights to all human beings must fail, however. The first is relatively simple. It is that not everyone wishes that they should continue to enjoy the same moral protections were they to become senile. It is common for people to say, indeed, (especially as the prospect of senility becomes increasingly real) that they only hope that someone has the nerve to kill them off quickly once they reach that state. The second reason for failure is more deeply metaphysical. It is, that it is doubtful whether personal identity can be preserved through cognitive changes as massive as the slide into senility. Although at the end of such a change the very same human being (or physical body) would still exist, of course, it is highly doubtful whether *I* would any longer exist.

For the resulting human being would have none of the same beliefs, desires, interests, memories, or qualities of character that – arguably – constitute my identity as a person.[4] This, too, accords with ordinary parlance. It is common for people to say of their friends or relatives in such circumstances, such things as 'It is not really Granny in that hospital ward, any longer.' But if, following the slide into senility, the resulting person is not me, then I cannot now *self-interestedly* reject rules that affect that person. Yet this is what I would have to be able to do, if the senile are to be accorded moral standing, on this approach.

SLIPPERY SLOPES AND SOCIAL STABILITY

There is a very different way in which contractualists, of whatever variety, can attempt to secure direct moral rights for all human beings. As with Rawls's suggestion, this one, too, will leave animals without moral standing. The strategy depends upon the fact that there are no sharp boundaries between a baby and an adult, between a not-very-intelligent adult and a severe mental defective, or between a normal old person and someone who is severely senile. The argument is then that the attempt to accord direct moral rights only to rational agents (normal adults) would be inherently dangerous and open to abuse.

This is, of course, a version of slippery slope argument. The suggestion is that if we try to deny moral rights to some human beings, on the grounds that they are not rational agents, we shall be launched on a slippery slope which may lead to all kinds of barbarisms against those who *are* rational agents. It is important to be clear about the level on which this argument is supposed to operate, however. For there is nothing to stop us, at the level of theory, from insisting that only rational agents have rights, leaving a large range of cases in which possession of rights would be indeterminate. Or we could insist that possession of rights itself should be a matter of degree, the killing of a human being becoming more and more serious, in terms of direct infringements of right, as a baby gradually advances into adulthood. There would be nothing incoherent in these theories as such. The claim must be that it is in the application of these theories in the real world that the danger lies. The idea is that such theories would be inherently susceptible to abuse by unscrupulous people, and ought therefore not to be adopted.

In contrast, there really is a sharp boundary between human beings and all other animals. Not necessarily in terms of intelligence or degree of rational agency, of course – a chimpanzee may be more intelligent than a mentally defective human, and a dolphin may be a rational agent to a higher degree than a human baby. But there is not the same practical threat to the welfare of rational agents in the suggestion that all animals should be excluded from the domain of direct moral concern. Someone who argues that since animals do not have rights, therefore babies do not have rights, therefore there can be no moral objection to the extermination of Jews, Gypsies, gays, and other so-called 'deviants', is unlikely to be taken very seriously, even by those who share their evil aims.

This argument for according rights to all human beings does seem to have a good chance of success. For rational agents choosing moral principles to govern their behaviour should, of course, pay attention to the ways in which those principles might be distorted or abused. If the argument has a weakness, however, it lies in its empirical assumption – namely, that a rule according direct rights only to rational agents would be likely to be abused in such a way as to undermine itself. For provided that all understand the theoretical basis of the rules, they will be fore-armed against abuse. Thus, suppose it were generally agreed that all rational agents have moral rights, and that those who are not fully rational agents have rights in proportion to the extent of their rational agency. Then the reply is obvious to anyone who tries to argue that since babies do not have direct rights, and since there is no clear boundary between infancy and normal adulthood, therefore there can be no direct moral objection to the holocaust. It is that the gradual transition from infancy to adulthood is at the same time the transition from not bearing moral rights, to having them in full measure.

This attempt to undermine the argument from a slippery slope fails in its turn, however. For one of the facts that rational agents will know is that most people are not very deeply theoretical. They should therefore select moral principles that will provide a stable and easily understood framework within which ordinary people can debate questions of right and wrong. Seen in these terms, a rule that accorded rights in proportion to degree of rational agency *would* be wide open to creeping abuse. For to think and speak in terms that withhold moral rights from some human beings is to invite people to try to draw yet further distinctions – for example, withholding rights from those who are sexually or intellectually 'deviant', or from those whose intelligence is low. So I conclude that our slippery slope argument is indeed successful in according rights to all human beings.

It is worth noting the differences between the argument sketched here, and Regan's superficially similar argument for treating human babies as if they had rights.[5] Recall that for Regan, those who have moral rights are primarily those who are subjects-of-a-life – that is, who have a sense of their own future and their own past. He then realises that on such an account human babies, up to the age of one, at least, will not count as having rights. His reply is that we should, nevertheless, treat such babies *as if* they had the same rights as everyone else, by way of encouraging a moral climate in which the rights of individuals are taken seriously. The first point to make about Regan's proposal is that it does not succeed in according rights to human babies. To say that we should treat babies *as if* they had rights is not the same as saying that they *do* have rights. Yet it is this stronger conclusion that we were able to deliver by means of the slippery slope argument outlined above. The second point is that it is, in any case, by no means clear how Regan's argument is supposed to go. That is, it is far from clear how treating those who do not have rights as if they did have them would foster a climate in which the rights of individuals are taken seriously. The only obvious suggestion is that any moral system in which some human beings are denied moral rights is liable, by creeping abuse, to lead to a situation in which some of those who do have moral rights have their rights ignored. This is, in effect, our slippery slope argument, only shorn of its contractualist context. The very argument that for Regan leads to the conclusion that we should treat all humans *as if* they had rights, for a contractualist leads to the conclusion that they *do* have rights. This is, I think, to the advantage of the latter.

Would a slippery slope argument for according direct moral rights to all human beings at the same time rule out abortion? For there is no clear line between foetus and baby, any more than there is a clear line between baby and adult. But in fact the issues here are not the same. For one of the things that contracting rational agents should consider seriously, in framing their rules, are the natural responses of thought and feeling that antecede moral belief. (This point will come to the fore in Chapter 7.) It is natural to be struck by the suffering of senile old people or babies, in a way that both supports and is supported by assigning direct rights to these groups. It is not so natural for us to respond similarly towards a foetus, however, especially in the early stages, unless we already have prior moral beliefs about its status. A rule withholding moral rights from foetuses, and hence permitting at least early abortions, may therefore be quite easily defended against abuse. This will become clearer in the chapter after next.

In addition to the argument from a slippery slope outlined above, contractualists have available one further argument for according moral standing to all human beings. This is an argument from social stability. One thing that rational contractors should certainly consider, in framing a basic set of principles, is whether those principles would have the desired effect of facilitating a stable, co-operative, community. In this they should have regard, among other things, to the known facts of human psychology. One such fact is that human beings are apt to care as intensely about their offspring as they care about anything, irrespective of age and intelligence. A rule withholding moral standing from those who are very young, very old, or mentally defective is thus likely to produce social instability, in that many people would find themselves psychologically incapable of living in compliance with it.

It might be replied that stability could equally well be

achieved by a rule requiring us to respect the legitimate concerns of others. Then all those non-rational humans who are objects of love would receive protection after all, out of respect for the feelings of those who love them. But this is inadequate. It would only accord such humans the same protection as items of property. Just as I am obliged not to damage or destroy your cherished Mercedes, so I should be obliged not to damage or destroy your child. But such obligations may be overridden in cases where more fundamental rights are at stake. Suppose, for example, that your Mercedes blocks the entrance to a mine-shaft in which I have become imprisoned. You have become accustomed to use the entrance as a garage during the week, and I should face a five-day wait to get out. Then I may surely destroy the car if this is my only means of escape, no matter how much you may care about it, and even though my life may be in no danger. In these circumstances you would, surely, accept that I had acted reasonably. But no one could bring themselves to accept with equanimity the destruction of their child in a similar situation. The only way of framing rules that we can live with, then, is to accord all human beings the same basic rights – that is to say, moral standing.

A REPLY FROM ANTHROPOLOGY

In reply to both of the above arguments, it may be objected that there have been many human societies that have not accorded the same basic rights to all human beings, and yet that have been both stable and in other respects civilised – no slippery slope was ever embarked upon. There have been very many human communities in which infanticide has been widely practised as a means of population control, for example.[6] Yet the members of these communities were in all other ways inclined to show at least as much respect for human life as ourselves, and were tender and loving towards those children who were allowed to survive. So, it may be claimed, it is simply not true that a system of morality that only accords moral standing to those human beings who are rational agents need in any way be self-defeating, or have dire consequences.

This objection fails, however, for a variety of reasons. First, all the communities in which infanticide has been openly practised have been traditional ones, with the practices in question sanctioned by long-standing social custom, and often by religious belief as well. Such methods of achieving social stability are no longer available to us. In our modern world, moral rules have to be defensible in the face of free and open discussion, without appeal to religious sanction. In order to show that all human beings should be accorded the same basic rights, I do not have to argue that a rule withholding moral standing from some human beings would be disastrous in all circumstances. It is enough that it would be disastrous for us.

Second, almost all the communities in question were teetering on the edge of survival, either existing in particularly harsh environmental conditions, or in areas where productive land was in short supply. Infanticide was thus deemed necessary to prevent general starvation, or to preserve the lives of older children. It is, then, by no means obvious that these communities failed to recognise the moral standing of human infants. Their acts of infanticide may rather be assimilated to legitimate cases of killing in self-preservation. Any version of contractualism will surely allow such killing, as the following example will make clear.

Suppose that Doris and Diana are deep sea divers, whose diving bell has come adrift and sunk to the bottom of an ocean trench. They are told by radio that they cannot hope to be rescued for at least twelve hours. They have only six hours of oxygen remaining. So at least one of them must die. Now suppose, additionally, that Diana in any case depends for her survival upon Doris (just as a human infant depends for its survival upon adults) – perhaps she needs Doris to administer a life-saving injection after ten hours, that she cannot administer herself. In these circumstances it is surely permissible that Doris should kill Diana in order that she herself may survive. While it may be admirable of Doris if she were to volunteer to die along with Diana, this cannot be morally required of her. That she should be prepared to kill in these circumstances need not mean denying that Diana has moral standing or, indeed, violating her rights. For rational contractors ought surely to allow that in those rare cases where all will die unless one is killed, it is legitimate to preserve oneself. Then so, too, in the case of infanticidal communities – their actions may be consistent with according full moral standing to infants.

The third reason why the anthropological evidence fails to undermine the slippery slope and social stability arguments outlined earlier involves a distinction between the general virtues of justice and beneficence, which is in any case central to contractualism, as we shall see in Chapter 7. (Justice has to do with duties of non-interference, beneficence with attachment to the welfare of others.) Suppose that human infants are accorded full moral standing, on a par with normal adults. Then the fact that they are incapable of surviving on their own means that the actions necessary to keep them alive are required by beneficence rather than justice. It need not infringe a person's rights if we fail to keep them alive, though it may display a serious lack of generosity on our part. But in circumstances where the costs to us would be severe (as they would be in most of the cases we are considering), our failure to keep alive need not even show this. Recall the example of callous Carl from Chapter 2, who failed to save the child drowning in a pond. His action would surely appear in quite a different light if he were rushing his own child to hospital for an emergency operation. That he fails to show beneficence towards the drowning child in such circumstances involves no violation of right, nor need it involve any sort of denial that the child has full moral standing. This example looks entirely parallel to the cases of the infanticidal communities we have been considering.

Since the anthropological objection fails, I conclude that contractualists have at least two successful strategies for according direct moral rights to all human beings. The only problem still facing contractualism, therefore, is to get closer to common-sense attitudes towards animals. For the intuition that Astrid would act wrongly in using her cat as a dart-board is a powerful one. I shall return to the matter in Chapter 7. First, I shall spend a chapter considering the extent to which it is true that animals should not be counted as rational agents, as I have been assuming up to now. For if it were to turn out that most animals are rational agents after all, then reflective equilibrium would in any case have been attained. Since it is clear that only prejudice can stand in the way of assigning the same basic rights to all who are rational agents, we should have found an explanation for why Astrid is wrong to throw darts at her cat.

SUMMARY

No version of contractualism will accord moral standing to animals. There may, nevertheless, be indirect duties towards animals, owed out of respect for the legitimate concerns of animal lovers. But the protection thus extended to animals is unlikely to be very great. Nor can this approach explain the common-sense intuition that unmotivated cruelty to an animal is directly wrong. Contractualists also face the challenge of extending direct moral rights to those human beings who are not rational agents. While the first two avenues discussed, through which contractualists might hope to grant such rights, were seen to fail, two others – a slippery slope argument and an argument from social stability – proved successful.

CHAPTER 6

Animals and rational agency

In this chapter I shall consider how much truth there is in the simplifying assumption made throughout Chapter 5 – namely, that no animals are rational agents in the sense that would be necessary to ensure that they have moral standing within contractualism.

CLEVER HANS AND THE SPHEX WASP

Plainly there is no problem of principle about animals being rational agents – whatever, precisely, the relevant sense of 'rational agent' might turn out to be (this will be investigated as we go along). For example, if the story I told in Chapter 3 of the university educated apes had turned out to be true – or, indeed, if almost any story from children's literature, such as Richard Adams's *Watership Down*,[1] were to turn out to be true – then it is clear that the animals involved would be rational agents. Our question is one of fact, not of principle. We are to consider whether there is sufficiently good reason for thinking that any animals *are* rational agents. I shall begin with two (true) tales designed to illustrate the pitfalls involved in interpreting animal behaviour.

Clever Hans was a horse who lived in the late nineteenth century, who was widely believed to be able to count. If an array of objects was placed before him, and he was asked how many there were, Hans would stamp his hoof the appropriate number of times. There seemed to be no question of cheating. His trainer could not have been giving him covert signals, for example, since Hans would perform equally well whether or not his trainer was present. But then it was discovered that if the only people present were, themselves, unable to count, or if they were so positioned that they could not see the objects to be counted, then Hans did not know when to stop – he just went on stamping his hoof. What had been happening was that Hans had been responding to subtle behavioural changes in his audience, such as a slight intake of breath, when the audience knew that he had reached the right number. Without these changes, he was lost.

Now, the moral of this story is not that Hans's behaviour was entirely unintelligent. On the contrary, it did display intelligence of a sort, only not the kind originally attributed to him. He had learned to recognise and respond to a variety of subtle behavioural changes, rather than to count. The real moral is that we need to be cautious in interpreting animal behaviour in experiments that require animals to interact with human beings. For it is hard to be sure that we have not been unwittingly encouraging the animals to do what we want, by conditioning them to respond to unconscious human signals. Many of the experiments that have claimed to be able to teach chimpanzees to use an articulate sign language, for example, are infected with this problem.[2]

Now consider the story of the Sphex wasp. The female of the species lays her eggs in a burrow, leaving them to hatch on their own. Before she abandons her eggs, however, she captures and paralyses a cricket, and brings it to the burrow where she leaves it to provide fresh food for her young when they hatch. Before taking the cricket into the burrow, she places it on the ground outside and goes in alone, apparently to check for intruders. She then emerges to drag the cricket inside, leaving it close to her eggs. All this seems remarkably intelligent – indeed, an example of long-term planning and foresight. This appearance, however, is an illusion. If the cricket is moved by an experimenter very slightly while she is in the burrow, she will re-emerge, drag the cricket back to its original position outside the entrance, and then re-enter the burrow alone once more. This cycle of behaviour can be repeated dozens of times. What looked like intelligent behaviour turns out to have been *rigid* – presumably a pre-programmed action pattern.

The moral of this story is that it is not enough, if we are to show that an animal is intelligent, to show that the direction of its behaviour may be characterised as intelligent, being such as to fulfil the creature's long-term needs. In order to count as exhibiting genuine intelligence, the behaviour must also be appropriately flexible. It must display sensitivity to changes in the environment in a way that suggests beliefs are being formed, up-dated, and acted upon.

THE ANTHROPOMORPHIC TENDENCY

The stories above bear emphasising, because we have a pervasive tendency towards anthropomorphic interpretations of animal behaviour. There are two sources of this, one of which is culture-specific, but one of which is, arguably, universal. I shall consider each of them briefly in turn.

Many cultures tell stories in which animals act out human roles. But in our Western culture the literature and enter-tainment directed at young children has been almost entirely monopolised by anthropomorphic treatments of animals. There is hardly a children's story, nowadays, that does not have an animal as its central character, engaging in human-like projects, and exhibiting patterns of thought and feeling that are distinctively human. It is surely inevitable that all this covert propaganda in childhood should have an effect in later life – if not actually encouraging a belief that animals entertain conscious thoughts just like ours (a belief that may seem surprisingly widespread), at least reinforcing a tendency to seek explanations for animal behaviour in terms of rational planning for long-term goals. This is not to say, of course, that all such explanations are false – only that we should be on our guard against attributions of intelligence that go beyond what the behavioural evidence would really warrant.

No doubt the anthropomorphic tendency derives partly from facts about our culture. But it also seems to me to have sources that go much deeper, grounded in the very structure of human cognition, as I shall now try to explain. One relevant claim here is that our knowledge of the psychology of our own species is very probably innate, having been selected for in evolution because of its decisive advantages in ensuring our survival.[3] A number of considerations support this claim. One is that our common-sense psychology is highly complex, but is acquired by young children within the space of a very few years.[4] Yet children are never explicitly taught it, and it is hard to see how they could learn it for themselves, since most of the phenomena with which it deals – people's thoughts, feelings, and decisions – are hidden from casual observation. (While young children may be supposed to have access to the occurrence of such phenomena in themselves, through introspection, this cannot be the source of their knowledge of the causal relationships between those states, which is what the bulk of common-sense psychology is concerned with.) Another consideration is that knowledge of common-sense psychology must be presupposed before co-operation and communication can take place. If you had no knowledge of beliefs and desires and the characteristic manner in which they interact, then, plainly, you could neither co-operate with others, nor understand what they said to you. It would hardly be surprising, therefore, if knowledge of common-sense psychology should turn out to be innate, given the crucial role of both co-operation and communication in human survival.

Another relevant claim to have emerged recently is that common-sense psychology provides the source for one of our most basic explanatory strategies. One body of evidence supporting this claim derives from studies of primate behaviour, which suggest that the driving force behind the evolution of human intelligence was distinctively *social* intelligence, not technical intelligence as has often been believed.[5] Another source of evidence comes from studies of child concept acquisition, which suggest that the basic conceptual repertoire of young children includes the concepts of common-sense psychology. These concepts are initially over-extended, being applied well beyond their proper domain, until more varied explanatory strategies are learned.[6]

Put the above claims together, and what you get is the thesis that it is an innately determined aspect of human cognition that explanation in terms of beliefs, thoughts, and desires forms one of our most basic explanatory strategies. Other things being equal, we tend to try to explain a given phenomenon in terms of attributions of intelligence, having a natural tendency to offer such explanations until the evidence forces us to think otherwise. This is certainly consistent with the impulse towards animistic explanations of natural phenomena, such as storms and earthquakes, common amongst primitive peoples. So what follows, again, is that we need to tread carefully in interpreting animal behaviour, taking care that we are not tempted to attribute intelligence beyond what the evidence will allow.

ANIMAL BELIEVERS

Whatever else a rational agent may be, it is, plainly, a creature that has beliefs, and acts on them to satisfy its desires. Our common-sense view would certainly be that beliefs and desires may be attributed to most species of animal, including all mammals, as well as many birds, reptiles, and amphibians (though it would not be correct to attribute them to insects, if the points made in Chapter 3 were sound). We say of the dog who leaps up at the familiar sound of his owner's car, for example, and begins scratching excitedly at the door, that he believes his owner to have returned home. And we say of the cat creeping carefully round the side of a bush, that she believes the bird to be behind it. Such explanations of animal behaviour (and also, to some extent, the corresponding predictions) seem remarkably successful. This creates a powerful presumption that many species of animal are, indeed, truly believers. This may be further reinforced by recalling the claim defended in Chapter 3 – that all mammals and birds, at least, should be counted as genuinely sentient – together with the facts on which that claim was based, namely the extensive similarities in behaviour, and of brain structure and function, between such animals and ourselves.

There have been a number of arguments to the contrary,

however.[7] Many of these are in fact weak, or make eminently deniable assumptions – taking for granted, for example, without further argument, that all beliefs and desires must be expressed in natural language. Perhaps the most powerful of these arguments, however, are those due to Donald Davidson, and they have also been very influential.[8] I propose to consider the two main ones. The first of these is, in outline, this: in order to have beliefs at all you must possess, in addition, the concept of belief; but in order to possess the concept of belief, in turn, you must have a language; in which case it will follow that non-linguistic creatures cannot have beliefs.

Davidson has defended the premisses of this argument rather differently in different publications. Consider first the claim that having beliefs requires you to possess the concept of belief. In 'Thought and Talk' he tries to defend this by claiming that having a belief requires understanding the possibility of being mistaken, which requires, in turn, a grasp of the contrast between true belief and false belief. Now, the latter claim is undeniable. But why should we grant the former? No reason for it is given, and it is hard to see what such a reason might be. For why should there not be simple, but genuine, kinds of belief where all beliefs are treated as certainties (without even the possibility of thought of a mistake) until they are eradicated by conflicting evidence that overwhelms them? In 'Rational Animals', on the other hand, Davidson argues that having a belief requires the possibility of being surprised, which involves, in turn, the belief that your original belief was false. Presumably the thought here is that it would be unintelligible that you should, while retaining a particular belief, just carry on as before when confronted with the fact that it is false (that is, with a contradictory belief). This may be true, but does not establish the point. For to say that any organism with beliefs must have cognitive mechanisms for identifying and resolving conflicts of belief is not to imply that the organism need be capable of *thinking about*, or have any concept of, its own beliefs. And it is difficult to see why this latter claim should be true.

Since we have rejected the first premiss of Davidson's argument, we have already done enough to avoid the conclusion. But let us consider, in any case, how he tries to defend the further claim that possession of the concept of belief requires language. In 'Thought and Talk' he argues that the concept of belief is only acquired in connection with the activity of interpreting the speech of others. But this just begs the question at issue, given that we also employ the concept of belief in explaining the non-verbal behaviour of both animals and ourselves. And it is unlikely, moreover, that the concept of belief is one that we have to acquire at all. Rather that concept is, plausibly, a component in a theory of the mind (common-sense psychology) that we know innately.[9] In 'Rational Animals', on the other hand, Davidson argues that the concept of belief presupposes the concept of objective truth, which presupposes, in turn, the concept of inter-subjective, communicable, truth. But these claims are again undefended, yet are highly contentious. For example, why would not a thought, by description, of the way things are irrespective of what I may take to be the case, be sufficient for a concept of objective truth? Yet such a thought need not presuppose that I am a potential communicator or language user.

Davidson's other main argument against animals having beliefs is again a sophisticated defence of the claim that beliefs cannot really be possessed by any creatures that are not users of language. The argument is that, in the absence of language, we cannot draw the sorts of fine distinctions amongst beliefs necessary for them to have genuine *intentionality*. But all this will take some explaining.

First, the concept of intentionality in philosophy is a technical one, although the phenomenon it picks out is easily recognised. (Note that this technical use of 'intentional' applies primarily to beliefs and other representational mental states, including intentions. In contrast, in the everyday sense it is primarily overt actions that are intentional – meaning that they are caused in the usual way by beliefs, desires, and intentions.) Intentional states are distinctive in that they contain representations of things that may or may not exist, and represent them in one way rather than another. Someone can believe, or hope, that Atlantis once supported a great civilisation, although there is, in reality, no such place. In contrast, if there is no such place as Atlantis then it is impossible for anyone to go there. So belief, but not physical travel, can put you in relation to a non-existent thing. Moreover, someone can believe that there is water in the jug without believing that there is H_2O in the jug, even though water *is* H_2O; and someone can believe that Mr Hyde is the murderer without believing that Dr Jekyll is, even though Jekyll *is* Hyde; and so on. In contrast, if water boils at 100 degrees, then so, too, must H_2O, and if Hyde is thirty-two years old, then so, too, must Jekyll be. So the property of belief, but not the properties of boiling point or age, can apply differently to one and the same thing, depending on how that thing is represented in the description of it.

Now Davidson's argument is that these fine-grained distinctions amongst beliefs can only be drawn on the basis of evidence that is linguistic. Only if a creature can do something like *assert* that Hyde is the murderer while *denying* that Jekyll is, can we have reason for distinguishing the one belief from the other. And similarly, only if the creature can do something like respond to a request to fetch some water by bringing the jug, while failing to respond in the same way when asked to fetch some H_2O, can the belief that water is in the jug be distinguished from the belief that H_2O is in the jug. In which case those animals that lack an articulate language, as presumably almost all do, cannot be said to possess fine-grained beliefs. There is nothing that a dog can do, for example, that can make a difference between the statements 'Attila believes that his master is home', 'Attila believes that Mr Smith is home', and 'Attila believes that the president of the bank is home', provided that Attila's master is in fact Mr Smith, who is president of the bank. It can make no difference which description we use, no matter what Attila may do.

One response to this argument would be to allow that animals cannot have fine-grained beliefs (or, at least, that those without language cannot), but to insist that they may, nevertheless, have coarse-grained ones. To take this line would be to defend a notion of belief-content for animals according to which one and the same belief may be characterised indif-

ferently as 'the belief that my master is home', 'the belief that
Mr Smith is home', or as 'the belief that the president of the
bank is home'. But this would be the wrong move to make
against Davidson, since it would, in effect, concede to him that
animal beliefs lack intentionality. Yet to concede the intentionality of belief is to concede belief, since it is essential to the
very notion of belief that beliefs should represent things in one
way *rather than* another.

The correct response is not to claim that animal beliefs are
indeterminate between fine-grained descriptions, but rather to
insist that the sorts of descriptions canvassed above are *falsely*
attributed to animals. Very likely Attila does not have any
beliefs that can be characterised correctly using such terms as
'master', 'Mr Smith', or 'the president of the bank', since dogs
lack the requisite concepts. On the contrary, taking animal
beliefs seriously must involve trying to describe the way in
which *they* represent things. It seems plausible, for example, that
Attila will represent his master in terms of some schema of
appearance – some complex set of properties of sight, smell, and
voice. Equally, in place of our concept 'home' Attila may
employ something like the concept 'protectable territory'.
Then it will be straightforwardly false to describe Attila as
believing that his master is home. Rather, what Attila believes
will be something like 'The one who appears like *this* is on
protectable territory'. Needless to say, the ways in which
animals represent things will not be easily discoverable. But this
is no argument for saying that such modes of representation do
not exist.

Can this sort of approach to animal beliefs preserve for them
all the features of intentionality? Surely yes. Animals, like us,
can have beliefs in non-existent objects. Thus the dog who barks
wildly in the night when a lamp is blown over by the wind might
do so because of the belief that something is intruding on
protectable territory. And it ought to be easy enough to find
cases where a dog has contradictory beliefs about what is, in
fact, one and the same thing, by virtue of representing that
thing in two different ways. For example, suppose that Delia
always appears to Attila in one of two different guises – now

being recognised by smell (with her appearance disguised) and bringing food, now being recognised by appearance (with her smell disguised) and bringing rough treatment. Then Attila might easily manifest the beliefs that *this* person is a source of food while *that* person is not, although it is, of course, the same person in each case. There seems no essential difference between this, and the example that forms a paradigm of human intentionality, where someone believes that Hyde is the murderer while believing that Jekyll is not.

CATEGORISATION AND CONCEPTS

Attempts to argue that creatures lacking an articulate language cannot have beliefs, in advance of detailed consideration of the evidence, have been seen to fail. We therefore need to look at what animals can actually do, and how their abilities are best explained. And in fact, the evidence is overwhelming that almost all animals have cognitive abilities that go beyond mere connections of stimulus and response, of the sort beloved by behaviourists. Even goldfish can retain in short-term memory (for a period of about one minute) the location of previously discovered food.[10] However, although these abilities may be, in some sense, genuinely cognitive, this does not mean that they must involve beliefs and desires – which is what we need if animals are to stand any chance of counting as rational agents. This point will come out most clearly in the contrast between the ability to categorise things into two or more classes, and possession of a genuine concept, as I shall now try to explain.

Pigeons, for example, are capable of learning remarkably sophisticated perceptual discriminations. They can learn to categorise slides depending on whether those slides contain a triangle or not, or depending on whether they contain a human being (in whatever pose) or not, and so on.[11] They can soon come to peck at the slide to gain a reward only if it contains a triangle, or a human being. But do the pigeons thereby possess the concept of a triangle, or of a human appearance? Being able to sort things into categories, in a series of yes/no choices, is surely different from having a concept. For a machine can categorise potatoes by weight or size without, of course, possessing any concepts of weight or size. But what more is needed? Well, plainly, if something is to possess a concept it must be capable of having beliefs or desires in which that concept figures. Now, this might not seem to take us very far, beyond explaining why it is that the potato-sorting machine possesses no concepts. For, after all, what we started off wanting to know was whether pigeons may be said to possess beliefs. But in fact the answer is useful, in two respects.

First, it is essential to the very notions of belief and desire, that beliefs and desires are states that interact with one another to produce behaviour. In fact, genuine attributions of belief and desire go along with a certain standard for explaining behaviour, which I call the practical-reasoning-model. On this account, to explain an item of behaviour is to exhibit it as the consequence of a piece of practical reasoning, of the form 'If I do X then I shall get Y, and I want to get Y, so I shall do X'. (It need not be assumed that the reasoning process in question is a conscious one, in animals any more than in ourselves. What is crucial for the application of the practical-reasoning-model is only that there should be states of belief and desire that interact together to produce an intention in the way the structure of practical reasoning outlines.) It follows, then, that pigeons possess the concept of a triangle only if they exhibit patterns of behaviour that are best explained using the practical-reasoning-model, by attributing to them beliefs and desires within the content of some of which, at least, the concept of a triangle figures.

Second, it is essential to beliefs and desires that they should be structured out of elements that can be recombined with others. The concepts that fit together to make up the content of any given belief or desire must be capable of fitting together with other concepts to form yet other contents. Any creature capable of believing that grass is green, for example, must be capable of believing that grass is something else (edible, perhaps), and of believing that something else is green (emeralds, say).

For these reasons, it is doubtful whether a child who can sort bricks into red and green, but can do nothing else involving those colours, as yet possesses the concepts of red and green. When the child begins to form beliefs such as that green apples are sour, red ones sweet; that red things are often hot; that green lights mean go, red ones mean stop; and so on, *then* it will possess the concepts of red and green. In the same way, we should not attribute the concept of a triangle, or of a human appearance, to a pigeon, unless we are prepared to take seriously explanations of its behaviour on the practical-reasoning-model. (For example, 'Pecking at triangles is a way of getting food. I want food. Here is a triangle. So I shall peck at it.') And we should only take these sorts of explanations seriously, where the pigeon's behaviour displays sufficient flexibility for us to be able to attribute to it a variety of different contents involving the concept of a triangle.

While these points may make it doubtful whether pigeons have beliefs (or, at least, beliefs about triangles), they do nothing to undermine the attribution of beliefs to most, if not all, species of mammal. For we surely do take seriously the use of the practical-reasoning-model to explain their behaviour. For example, we might explain the behaviour of a dog by attributing to it the sequence: 'I want to get the ball. The ball is on the table. If I jump on to the chair I can reach the table. So I shall jump on to the chair.' Moreover, a dog's behaviour certainly exhibits a wide variety of ways in which it can interact with a ball – fetching, chewing, chasing, and catching – suggesting that the concept of a ball does form a component in a number of different canine beliefs and desires.

ANIMAL PLANNERS

I propose to grant that all mammals have beliefs and desires. They form beliefs about their immediate environment on the basis of their perceptions, and are able to act in the light of those beliefs to satisfy their immediate desires. Still, this is by no means enough for these animals to count as rational agents. For recall that rational agents, in the context of contractualism, are required to agree with one another on the rules to govern all of their future interactions. They must therefore be capable of representing in thought a variety of long-term futures, and of making rational choices between those futures. So to count as a rational agent, an animal must not only be capable of acting to satisfy its immediate desires, but also of constructing and following a long-term plan. For our purposes, rational agents are planners.

In order to count as a rational agent, of course, you do not have to act rationally on every occasion. To say that normal adult humans are rational agents is not to imply that they never make mistakes, or construct thoroughly muddled plans. It implies only that they are capable of representing different possible futures, of working out which one they want, and of constructing some sort of plan to achieve the future that they desire. It is enough that they are capable of engaging in these activities at all, not that they perform them successfully, let alone superlatively. While rational agents are planners, they do not have to be very good planners.

It might be said, then, that plenty of animals should be counted as rational agents. Think of squirrels who store nuts in the autumn, birds who migrate south for the winter or build elaborate nests for the protection of their young, and of dogs who bury bones for later retrieval and consumption. Surely these are all cases of long-term planning? But in fact, to say that an animal engages in behaviour adapted to meet a predictable future eventuality is not to say that the animal has itself predicted that future, or arrived at its behaviour as a result of a plan. (Remember the Sphex wasp.) For it is left open that the behaviour in question may be merely an acquired habit, or that it may be innately determined. For example, it might be written into the genes of certain species of birds that they are to fly at a particular orientation relative to the stars when the sun reaches a certain position in the sky. This would not be planning, but reacting. (Indeed, the nut-burying behaviour of the European red squirrel, at least, is an innately determined action pattern that the squirrel will continue to perform in captivity, on a solid floor with no earth to dig.)[12]

There are at least two general reasons for thinking that none of the sorts of animal activities mentioned above manifest genuine planning. The first is that the skills involved in planning are transferable. These include the abilities to represent and predict future states of affairs, and to work out ways of bringing about or preventing those states of affairs. So if any animals were planners, it would be remarkable that they do not do more of it. If a dog were really capable of predicting that unless its food is hidden it may be stolen by others, and of working out that burying the food would keep it out of sight and smell until needed, then it is strange that it should not make use of these abilities in other areas of its life. Why, for example, do dogs never lay out food as bait for an unwary cat? Another way to put the point is this. It is distinctive of human beings, and a mark of our rational agency, that we can adapt to almost any circumstance or habitat. No other single animal species even begins to approximate to this adaptability. To the extent that this is so, it suggests that no other species of animal approximates to the status of a rational agent.

The second reason for doubting whether the activities of squirrels, birds, and dogs manifest genuine planning, is that it would then be remarkable that members of the same species should not come up with alternative plans. It seems essential to the activity of planning, as we understand it, that there will always be a number of possible ways of trying to achieve a given objective, even if not all of those ways would be equally successful. It would then be strange, if squirrels were engaging in genuine planning when they gather nuts, that some individuals should not hit upon the alternative plan of observing where other squirrels have hidden their nuts, and later stealing them. And if birds were really planning for the future of their offspring in building a nest, it would be strange that members of the same species should not hit upon alternative modes of construction, or that some individuals should not avoid the labour of building altogether by laying their eggs in the nests of others, as does the cuckoo. (The cuckoo, presumably, does this innately.)

Long-term planning implies more than mere possession of beliefs about the remote future, of course, or the ability to predict future states of affairs. It must also involve possession of long-term desires, which serve to set the ultimate goals for any prolonged projects undertaken. Since many of the putative examples of animal planning are concerned with individual survival, this may be the point at which we should consider the question deferred from Chapter 4 – namely, whether any animals may be said to have desires for their own future existence.

Possessing a desire implies possession of its constituent concepts. So a desire for one's own future existence must involve concepts of oneself, of the future, and of existence. Moreover, possession of any given concept must involve, in addition, possession of its contrasting concepts. To possess the concept of existence you must also possess the concept of non-existence. So if any animal were really capable of conceptualising, and desiring, its own future existence, it would also have to be capable of conceptualising *non*-existence. But there is no evidence that any animals are capable of this. True enough, if a dog returns to the spot where it had buried its bone to find the bone gone, it may express surprise. But there is nothing in this to manifest the thought that the bone has ceased to exist, rather than that it has been moved. Indeed, since a dog in such circumstances will generally hunt around the surrounding area before finally losing interest, it would seem to be the latter idea that is entertained, rather than the former. Of course, a human being in such a situation may behave similarly, at least initially. If I return to my desk to find my diary has disappeared from its usual position, I may begin by searching in the drawers and on the floor. But, in contrast to the dog, I can also manifest the belief that the diary has ceased to exist – for example, by accusing my secretary of having dropped it in the shredding machine by mistake.

There is a sense in which all animals will struggle for survival, of course, in that they will respond to perceived threats with aggression or fear. But this does not mean that they have desires for their own future existence, as opposed to non-existence. It only shows, at most, that they have desires to avoid damage or danger, which are conceptually simpler. All animals can make some distinction between things that are safe and things that are not, or between things that may damage them and things that will not. Some animals may, in addition, show sufficient variety in their behaviour for us to attribute to them possession of the corresponding concepts. But none of this shows that animals can have desires for their own future existence. Indeed, I assume that such desires should be denied of them.

In conclusion, many species of animal engage in short-term planning, if we take seriously the attribution of beliefs and desires to them. Consider the cat stalking a bird, or the dog jumping up on a chair to get a ball from the table. But this is not enough for the animals in question to be counted as rational agents, in the sense that matters for contractualism. This also requires long-term planning. But so far as I can see, no suggested animal behaviours are at all convincing as examples of long-term planning. Moreover, this is, in any case, by no means the only obstacle to counting any animals as rational agents. To be so counted, animals would also have to be capable of planning for the results of implementing social rules, as we shall see in the next section.

ANIMAL DECEIVERS

In order to have the kind of intelligence necessary to be a rational contractor, it is not enough to have beliefs and desires, and to be able to construct long-term plans in the light of those beliefs and desires. You must also have an idea of what it is to act under a general rule, and of what it might be like if all were to act under the same rule. This will require that you have a conception of the beliefs and desires of others, and that you are able to work out what might be expected of those others in particular cases if the rule in question were implemented. So rational agency requires, not just beliefs and desires, but beliefs about beliefs and desires – second-order beliefs, in fact. Is there any evidence that animals are capable of entertaining second-order beliefs?

The clearest way in which an animal can manifest second-order beliefs is by deceit. For to act deceitfully is to act in such a way as to induce intentionally a false belief in another. But if such action can be intentional, it must presuppose a conception of the beliefs of the other. So, do any animals engage in intentional deceit? There is anecdotal evidence that they do. For example, Donna's dog Dean likes to walk, and likes to sleep in Donna's armchair. One day when Donna is sitting comfortably in her chair, the dog lying awkwardly on the floor, Dean gets up and fetches his lead. But when Donna gets out of the chair to take the dog for a walk, Dean jumps up into the chair she has vacated. Did the dog not act with the intention of inducing in Donna the false belief that he wanted to go for a walk?

The trouble with this sort of anecdotal evidence is that it is always amenable to more neutral description, precisely because it is merely anecdotal. For example, we may re-describe the case above by saying that Dean wanted to walk and also wanted to lie in Donna's armchair. He set about trying to satisfy the first desire, but when, as an unintended consequence, the opportunity to satisfy the second arose, he set about doing that instead. All putative examples of deceptive behaviour in animals are, in principle, vulnerable to this sort of re-description.

In reply it might be said that there is very good reason why the evidence of deception in animals should be merely anecdotal. It is that deception, by its very nature, can only succeed if it is infrequent. Since there is always a real risk that a deception may be discovered and exposed, those who attempt to deceive others too often will soon find themselves without the opportunity to deceive at all, because no one will trust them. But this reply is only partially adequate. It can explain why the evidence of deception by any given individual animal should be merely anecdotal, but not why it should be so for the species as a whole. To make out a real case for intentional deception in animals, we should need frequent examples of apparent deception practised by different individual members of the same species. Such evidence (which would, as it were, be *systematically* anecdotal) is entirely lacking in connection with almost, but not quite, all species of animal. The exceptions are the great apes, particularly chimpanzees.

Studies of chimpanzee behaviour, both in captivity and the wild, are rife with examples such as the following. One ape, who is female, knows where a store of food is buried. But she also knows from past experience that if she goes directly to that store, then one particular larger male will follow her, and take it from her. So she sets off in the opposite direction, and begins to dig. When the male pushes her aside and takes over the digging for himself, she rushes back to the actual location to retrieve and consume the food. True enough, these tales are anecdotal, and cannot be reliably repeated. But taken together they constitute an impressive body of evidence.[13]

I propose to allow that chimpanzees, at least, have second-order beliefs about the beliefs and desires of others. But this is only a necessary condition of rational agency. It is by no means sufficient. In order to count as a rational agent, in the sense that matters for contractualism, an animal would also have to be capable of long-term planning, as we saw in the previous section. It would need, moreover, a conception of social rules, and of what it might be for all to act under the same social rules. Evidence of these aspects of rational agency would seem to be conspicuously absent, even in chimpanzees.

ANIMAL LANGUAGE

Bold claims have been made in recent years that chimpanzees, at least, count as rational agents in virtue of their capacity to use, and to understand, language.[14] Many animals use systems of signs of one sort or another, of course. Bees do a figure-of-eight dance to show the direction of nectar, dogs bark in warning and growl in threat, and birds sing to attract mates or to defend territory. But plainly this sort of thing is too far removed from human language to be of any interest in the current debate. For the behaviours in question are, very likely, innately determined action sequences, as well as lacking the structural complexity of human natural language. The claim made, however, is that chimpanzees can be taught to use signs in ways much more closely resembling our own.

The issue is important, because it does seem clear that full competence in the use of a human natural language (or something closely resembling it) would be a sufficient condition for a creature to count as a rational agent. Anything capable of using a system of signs with the expressive power of a human natural language must be able to use those signs with the intention of inducing beliefs in other users, and must therefore have second-order beliefs about those others' beliefs. Since such a creature must also be able to represent alternative futures, and the states of affairs on which those futures are contingent, it will be capable of long-term planning. Moreover, to have the expressive power of a human language, a system of signs must contain ways of representing various possible systems of rules, and the consequences of universal compliance with those rules. So a full language-user would be, without qualification, a rational agent, in the sense of the phrase that concerns us. In the light of the points made in earlier sections, indeed, it would seem that there can be no real prospect of showing any animals to be rational agents *except* by showing that they are capable of using an appropriately developed language. For there is little evidence of other sorts that even chimpanzees are capable of long-term planning, let alone that they are capable of conceptualising alternative systems of social rules. If we are to show that they are rational agents, our only remaining prospect is to show that chimpanzees are, at least potentially, language-users.

Many important criticisms have been made of the systems of signs taught to chimpanzees, even supposing that we set aside worries about the clever Hans phenomenon. Amongst these are that the sign-languages they have mastered show no significant syntax. In some cases there is no question, even, of the signs expressing articulate propositions, since only one sign is used at a time. But even in those cases where something like sentences are employed, it is in fact mere groupings of signs that are significant. Also, and relatedly, it has been objected that the systems taught to chimps are not genuinely productive, in the way that human natural languages are. We are capable, by virtue of our grasp of grammatical structure, of continually using old words in new ways, never before encountered, whereas the chimps are not. (You will, almost certainly, never before have come across the sentence 'A green dragon sleeps beneath my word-processor', for example. But now that you have confronted it, you will have no difficulty in grasping its meaning.) Finally, and perhaps most importantly, it has been pointed out that there is no evidence of the chimpanzees ever using their signs in thought, for solving problems or reasoning about what to do. They treat them merely as practical tools for enabling them to fulfil their immediate desires.[15]

More important than any of the above criticisms for our purposes, however, is the point that all the various systems of signs so far taught to chimpanzees have been concerned only with immediately perceptible aspects of the chimps' environment. Crucially, no chimpanzee has mastered the phenomenon of tense, or any way of representing particular future times. Nor have they mastered the concepts necessary for representing causality, conditionality ('if... then ... '), or general rules. But these concepts would be absolutely necessary if the chimps' mastery of language were to establish that chimpanzees should be counted as rational agents. For as we have seen, the capacities for long-term planning, and for considering the consequences of adopting certain general rules, are crucial to rational agency.

It is hardly surprising that attempts to teach languages to animals have met with such limited success. For as Noam Chomsky and others have forcefully argued, the human capacity for language is very likely an innately determined aspect of our cognition. In Chomsky's view, we ourselves are only able to learn languages because much information about the grammars of natural languages, as well as many linguistic concepts, are already contained in the inherited structure of our language faculty. Other animals, in lacking such a faculty, will find learning a full natural language impossible.[16]

As we saw earlier, the capacity to speak a full natural language would be a sufficient condition for a creature to count as a rational agent. It might additionally be wondered whether such a capacity is also a *necessary* condition of rational agency. This is not for the reason considered – and rejected – in a previous section, namely that possession of natural language is a necessary condition for having beliefs. It is rather because a rational agent, for our purposes, must be a possible rational contractor. Yet to enter into an explicit contract surely requires prior communication on the terms of the contract, and it seems clear that a languageless creature could not communicate anything so abstract as a proposed system of rules. This argument is, however, too swift. For consider the following example.[17] Suppose that we arrive on Mars to discover creatures that seem at least as intelligent as ourselves. They have a highly developed technology, and engage in activities that seem plainly to require long-term planning and knowledge of the beliefs and desires of others. But they lack any articulate system of communication. Perhaps the Martian creatures are extremely long-lived, and by nature solitary, in an environment that is by no means harsh. So they only need to meet one another to mate, and perhaps to exchange items of technology that each has developed independently.

In these circumstances it might be perfectly clear to us that the Martian creatures are rational agents. Could we, as contractualists, refuse to acknowledge that they have the same basic rights as ourselves, merely on the grounds that by being unable to communicate, they are incapable of entering into an explicit contract? I think not. As Scanlon remarks, the basic criterion, under contractualism, for whether or not a creature has moral standing is whether the idea of justification of a policy of action *to* that creature *makes sense*.[18] We do not actually have to be able to justify our system of rules to a creature, or some action under the rules, in order for it to have the same basic rights as ourselves. It is enough that the creature should have all the mental qualities and capacities necessary to appreciate such a justification, if it could somehow be transmitted. In fact, we ought to regard the Martian creatures' inability to communicate with others as a mere contingency that could conceivably be overcome without altering anything fundamental in their mode of cognition.

The above point generalises to cover any other qualities that might be necessary for a creature to be capable of entering into an explicit contract with us. Any creature incapable of making and keeping promises, for example, would not, in any meaningful sense, be able to enter into a contract. But this need not prevent it from having the status of a rational agent, if it were otherwise capable of long-term planning, and of working out the consequences of implementing alternative sets of social rules. For recall that the contract after which contractualism is named is hypothetical, not actual. We are not proposing to grant moral standing to creatures only after they have entered into a definite agreement with us. Rather, our moral rules will extend to those creatures provided that we might intelligibly attempt to justify our actions to them, in terms that none could reasonably reject who shared the aim of reaching free and unforced general agreement. The basis of contractualism lies in just this conception of reasonableness, not in any tit-for-tat contract.

HUMAN UNIQUENESS

No doubt rational agency, as such, admits of degrees. For the gradual development of a human infant, through childhood towards adulthood, is a process in which a fully-fledged rational agent slowly emerges, as we noted in Chapter 5. Yet I have been arguing, in effect, that no animals count as rational agents to any degree, since they lack even rudimentary versions of those qualities that are distinctive of rational agency. These are, namely, the capacities for long-term planning, for representing alternative sets of social rules, and for working out the likely consequences of implementing those rules. It therefore invites some comment that human beings should be unique in this respect. For we accepted in Chapter 3, after all, that human beings are continuous with the rest of the natural world, having evolved, like any other species of animal, through a process of natural selection. What follows are some highly speculative suggestions.

It may be our distinctive possession of an innately structured language faculty that underlies our uniqueness as rational agents. In the beginning, we may suppose, human beings came equipped with a working model of one another's psychology, somewhat as, perhaps, chimpanzees do today. Our ancestors' common-sense psychology might possibly have been more sophisticated than that possessed by chimpanzees, but would not have been different from it in kind. Given such a model, human beings would have been able to predict one another's behaviour, to a limited extent, and to engage in rudimentary forms of co-operative activity. The next – and crucial – development may have been the evolution of an innately structured language faculty. This would immediately have conferred decisive advantages in survival. It would have made it possible for human beings to co-ordinate their behaviour, and to frame and execute joint plans of action, to their mutual advantage. It would also have made it possible for early humans to begin exchanging information, and to pass on the accumulated wisdom of a society from generation to generation. But most importantly, for our purposes, it is possible that the evolution of such a language faculty facilitated a wider range for human thought. For, as Chomsky argues, there are essentially the same reasons for thinking that a wide range of human concepts are innate, as there are for thinking that knowledge of universal grammar is innate.[19] With the coming of language, and its associated grammatical forms, human beings could then frame thoughts about particular future times, about the long-term consequences of patterns of human behaviour, and agree rules with one another for the conduct of their affairs.

Whatever may be true of the hypothetical Martians considered earlier, it may thus be our unique status as natural language users that underlies our uniqueness, amongst creatures on earth, as rational agents. In which case it will also be our possession of natural language that accounts for the fact that human beings are alone in their moral standing, and in having direct rights, if the contractualist approach to morality is correct. Note, moreover, that this story has been told in terms that, so far from denying our continuousness with the rest of the natural order, presupposes it. There is substantial evidence that we do possess innate knowledge of common-sense psychology, and an innate language faculty, and it is easy to see why these faculties might have emerged through natural selection.[20] But if natural language is implicated in our capacity to represent future times, causes and conditionals, and general rules, then it will be our unique (but naturally explicable) possession of natural language that underlies our uniqueness as rational agents.

SUMMARY

Many animals may be said to have beliefs and desires. Some animals (particularly apes) may be said to have second-order beliefs and desires. But no animals possess the other qualities necessary for rational agency. Specifically, no animals appear capable of long-term planning, or of representing to themselves different possible futures. And no animals appear capable of conceptualising (let alone acting under) general socially agreed rules. I therefore conclude that the simplifying assumption made in Chapter 5 is correct. No animals count as rational agents, in the sense necessary to secure them direct rights under contractualism.

CHAPTER 7

Contractualism and character

In this chapter I shall confront the problem left over from Chapter 5, arguing that there is a way in which contractualism can accommodate duties towards animals that is independent of the question of offence caused to animal lovers. I shall then investigate just how extensive these duties may be, on the resulting account.

JUDGING BY CHARACTER

The general thesis I want to defend in this section from a common-sense perspective is that some actions are seriously wrong, not because they cause any harm or violate any rights, but simply because of what they reveal about the character of the agent. I shall later go on to argue that this thesis is not only correct, but fully explicable within contractualism. It will then turn out that some ways of treating animals are morally wrong, just as common sense tells us, but only because of what those actions may show us about the moral character of the agent. This will then be a form of indirect moral significance for animals that is independent of the fact that many rational agents care about animals, and hate to see them suffer.

Consider the example of Astrid, the astronaut, once again. Suppose, as before, that she has set her craft irreversibly to carry her out of the solar system, and that she is travelling with her cat and her grandfather. Now, at a certain point in the journey the grandfather dies. Out of boredom, Astrid idly cuts his corpse into bite-size pieces and feeds him to the cat. Is her action not morally wrong? It seems to me intuitively obvious that it is. But why? Plainly no harm is caused to the grandfather, nor is there anyone else who is to know of what she has done and be offended. Nor need the action violate any rights. For even if we allow that the dead have rights, such as might be infringed by ignoring someone's will, the grandfather may have waived all relevant rights in this case. Astrid may have heard him say many times, when he was still in full possession of his faculties, that he did not care in the least what happened to his corpse after his death. Even so, it seems to me that Astrid's action is morally wrong.

What Astrid does is wrong because of what it shows about *her*. Her action is bad because it manifests and expresses a bad quality of character, and it is an aspect of her character that is bad in the first instance. While there is perhaps no precise name for the defect of character that her action reveals, it might variously be described as 'disrespectful' or 'inhuman' – though each of these terms is really too broad for what is wanted. That she can act in the way she does shows either a perverse hatred of her grandfather in particular, or a lack of attachment to humanity generally.

It seems to be a universal feature of human nature that the treatment of corpses reflects something of our attitude towards the living. Certainly there are no human cultures that fail to have ceremonies of various sorts for honouring and disposing of the dead. Exactly what kinds of activities will count as honouring the dead is, of course, a highly conventional matter. In some cultures the proper way to dispose of a corpse is to bury it, in some to burn it, in some to embalm it, and in some to eat it. There might even be a culture in which the correct treatment of a corpse would be to cut it in pieces and feed it to a cat – though I am supposing that this is not true of Astrid's case. But in no cultures are corpses simply cast aside, as some might throw away a dead rabbit or a dead rose bush.

I propose that the manner in which we treat our dead is best understood symbolically, the corpse being an embodied image of the person who has died, and perhaps also an image of persons generally. If this is right, then an attack on a corpse would universally be interpreted as a symbolic attack on the dead person. It shows something about one's attitude to the individual person, and perhaps towards humanity generally, that one is prepared to attack their concrete image – that is to say, their corpse. Then if the attitudes revealed are bad ones, the actions that manifest and sustain them may be morally condemned as well.

Once we have realised that it is part of common-sense morality that an action can be criticised for what it shows about the character of the agent, we may begin to see that such judgements are really very common. For example, suppose that Jane is a doctor attending a medical conference who happens to be relaxing in the hotel bar in the evening with many of the other doctors present. The room is subdivided into a number of separate cubicles, in such a way that, while she can see the central area in front of the bar itself (which is currently empty), she cannot see any of the doctors seated in the other cubicles, although she knows that they are there. Suppose that she then notices someone walking across the central area, who collapses with what appears to be a heart attack. Out of laziness, Jane does not move to assist him. This is surely very wrong of her. But why?

Suppose that Jane's inaction does not in fact do any harm, since some of the other doctors are soon there to help. She had every reason to think that this would be the case, moreover, given that she knows there are many well-qualified and well-motivated people as close to the person as she is. Nor does she violate any rights by not going to the sick man's assistance. For while he may have a right to assistance from doctors in general, he has no special claim against her in particular. The only explanation is that Jane's inaction is wrong because of what it reveals about her character. It manifests a lack of humanity, more specifically a failure of beneficence. (Beneficence being the virtue that attaches us to the welfare of others.)

This is not to say that behaviour such as Jane's must always display lack of beneficence. If she happens to have a migraine at the time, or a twisted ankle, then her lack of action may easily be excusable. (It would be a different matter, of course, if Jane were to believe herself to be the only doctor present. Then even a migraine would be no excuse for inactivity.) There is a general truth here, that whether or not a given action manifests a particular defect of character will depend crucially on the circumstances, and the motives from which it is performed. Suppose that instead of being in a space-rocket, for example, Astrid had been adrift with her grandfather on a life-raft in the Atlantic. As before, the grandfather dies, and as before she cuts his corpse into small pieces. But now her motive is to use the pieces as bait to catch fish for her to eat. This makes a crucial difference. In such circumstances her treatment of his corpse need display no disrespect or inhumanity. For her own survival is at stake.

A CONTRACTUALIST RATIONALE

I have presented an intuitive case that actions may not only be judged for the harm that they cause or the rights that they infringe, but also for what they reveal about the character of the agent. Now recall from Chapter 2 how I argued that a utilitarian should take a serious interest in character – arguing, indeed, that qualities of character should be the primary object of utilitarian assessment. I also suggested in that chapter that contractualists should believe in a duty to develop in themselves a disposition towards beneficence – a point I shall return to shortly. But we have yet to achieve any general theoretical understanding of the way in which contractualists should regard qualities of character.

Why should rational agents who are trying to agree principles to govern their interaction with one another take any interest in character? Part of the answer lies in a realistic assessment of the springs of human action. While we are rational agents, in that we are capable of planning and evaluating alternative courses of action, most of our actions are by no means calculative. Some are routine, having passed the point where conscious deliberation is necessary any longer. Many others are done on the spur of the moment, prompted by circumstances in a way that pre-empts careful reasoning. Here general features of character, such as fair-mindedness or honesty, may make a great deal of difference to what we do. And even when there is time for deliberation it may require courage, for example, in order for us to pause for thought. (To take a fanciful case, if you find yourself in a room with a time-bomb, knowing that you have five minutes remaining until the explosion, courage may be displayed in pausing to reason that it would be better to take the bomb out into the garden, than to run into the garden yourself, leaving the bomb to destroy the house.) Indeed, the very readiness to take thought at all is itself a general feature of character, possessed by some people but not others.

In so far, then, as contracting rational agents are interested in the principles that are to govern their behaviour, they should also be interested in the general dispositions of thought and feeling that may make appropriate action more likely. So they should at least require people to try to develop those virtues that are sometimes described as 'enabling'. These include the virtues of courage, self-control, and thoughtfulness, that may be useful whatever it is you are trying to do, but also if you are trying to comply with moral rules. This is then one reason why rational agents should agree not just to accept certain rules, but also to try to develop certain features of character.

But what reason would rational contractors have for taking an interest in the specifically moral virtues, such as those of generosity, loyalty, friendliness, and honesty? Some of these are easy, in so far as they fall under the general category of justice. One would expect that rules requiring honest and open dealing and speaking, for example, would certainly be amongst those agreed upon. Then rational contractors, taking a realistic view of the springs of human action, should also require agents to develop a general love of, and disposition towards, honest action, rather than mere calculated compliance with the rule.

The reasons why contractualists should regard themselves as required to develop virtues of beneficence, such as generosity and loyalty, are more theoretically interesting. They arise out of the fact that rational agents should surely wish to agree on more than merely rules of non-interference. For they may be certain that they shall, at some point in their lives, require help from others. Most of us require assistance from others almost every day, indeed. This may take many different forms. It may be material, such as gifts or loans for those who find themselves temporarily without funds. Or it may be practical, in the form of physical assistance, for example, as when another pair of hands is necessary to lift something into place. Or it may be psychological, in the form of advice, friendship, sympathy, or support. A society in which rules of non-interference were respected, but in which no positive assistance was ever given, would not only be cold and cheerless, but many of our desires would remain unfulfilled as a result, and many of our most cherished projects would be incomplete.

Given that rational contractors should provide for duties of assistance, as well as those of non-interference, how should the former be instituted? Plainly such agents cannot agree that everyone has a duty to help each of those who are in need, in the way that they should agree that everyone has a duty to respect the autonomy of others. For the result would be incoherent. Suppose that my wallet has been stolen, for example, and that I need the bus-fare home. If *everyone* were to give me the fare, then I should be a millionaire! (It is no real reply to this, to say that as soon as one person has helped me, everyone else's duty to pay me the bus-fare lapses. For there will be many cases in which we are required to act in ignorance of what others may or may not have done.) Yet we cannot require only that everyone should give an appropriate proportion of what is needed, since many kinds of assistance are not divisible – as when the battery of my car is flat and I need someone to help me jump-start it.

For similar reasons, we cannot agree that those in need should have the *right* to assistance from others. For all rights imply a correlative duty. Sometimes, as in the case of the right not to be interfered with, the correlative duty is owed by all other agents – everyone is obliged not to infringe my autonomy. But then this would return us to the position we have just been discussing. Other rights imply duties on the part of particular persons or groups of persons. My right to fulfilment of a promise only implies a duty on the part of the promisor, for example, and my right to treatment of a minor illness only implies a duty on the part of the group of doctors with whom I am registered. But the problem with applying this model to the supposed right to assistance is to find some appropriate person or group of persons who owe the correlative duty. For example, just who would be supposed to owe me the duty of jump-starting my car? (Note that we cannot answer: 'The first person who *can* help me, who is aware of my need.' For then agents would not be able to know, in general, whether or not they owe the requisite duty. How are you supposed to be able to tell whether or not you are the *first* person to have become aware of my need who could help, without engaging in extensive investigation first?)

The obvious and only feasible solution is that rational agents should agree to develop a general *disposition* to help those in need, to be exercised when the opportunity arises to do so at no comparable cost to themselves. What they should agree to develop is a general attachment to the good of others, and a preparedness to act on their behalf. For if all have such an attachment, then almost everyone will get the help they need, when they need it (given certain obvious conditions of normality). Note that, in general, there will be no particular person whom I am obliged to assist. This will depend upon the circumstances, and on the other projects that I may be pursuing at the time. But each failure to help when the situation arises will count towards showing that I am not the sort of person I ought to be. However, those situations in which I am aware that I am the only person who *can* help, as in the example of callous Carl from Chapter 2, constitute a special case. Here failures to assist may encounter direct criticism – that Carl can walk on past the child in such circumstances is sufficient to show that he has not developed the right sorts of attachments, no matter whether he is late for work or has a horror of water.

Rational agents should thus agree to try to develop virtues of beneficence, because of their knowledge that all would wish to live in a community of a certain sort. If human beings are to flourish, they need the support and sympathy of those around them when they are struck down by illness, or poverty, or grief. They also need a sense of community with others that will require a degree of loyalty towards those who are close to them, and a general friendliness in their dealings with others. Rational agents should, therefore, agree not just to abide by certain rules and principles (not to kill, not to steal, not to cheat), but also to develop certain positive attachments and dispositions of feeling. They should agree that they may be criticised not just for infringing one another's rights, but also if they fail to show compassion and are not ready to help those who are in need.

It is important to stress a significant difference between the sort of contractualist treatment of character that has just been outlined, and the utilitarian approach to character presented in Chapter 2. In the context of utilitarianism, the value of virtues of character lies entirely in their consequences, leading to greater utility overall. Under contractualism, on the other hand, the consequentialist values of virtues of character – facilitating right action and contributing to a certain sort of society – enter in only at the stage when rational contractors are considering what sorts of persons they should try to become. Thereafter the rightness or wrongness of possessing, or failing to possess, a virtue of character is independent of such consequences. Thus in our example above, Astrid may be criticised for the failing of character displayed towards her grandfather's corpse even though, in the nature of the case, her faults will never again have any effect on her treatment of another human being. Rather, the criticism is that she has failed to do her fair share, in the moral sphere – like anyone else, she was obliged to try to create in herself the sort of moral character that would (in the right circumstances) contribute to the form of society that all would wish for. Utilitarians, in contrast, must deny that Astrid does anything wrong, since no harm of any sort will result.

ANIMALS AND CHARACTER

We can now explain, from a contractualist perspective, why it may be wrong of Astrid to use her cat as a dart-board, even though no other person will ever know or be distressed. Such actions are wrong because they are cruel. They betray an indifference to suffering that may manifest itself (or, in Astrid's case, that *might have* manifested itself) in that person's dealings with other rational agents. So although the action may not infringe any rights (cats will still lack direct rights under contractualism), it remains wrong independently of its effect upon any animal lover. Animals thus get accorded indirect moral significance, by virtue of the qualities of character that they may, or may not, evoke in us.

It is important to stress that right action with respect to animals, on this character-expressive account, will generally be non-calculative. People who act out of sympathy for the suffering of an animal do not do so because they calculate that they will become better persons as a result. Rather, their actions manifest an immediate sympathetic response, and are undertaken for the sake of the animals in question. For this is what having the right kind of sympathetic virtue consists in. This immediacy of response, however, is entirely consistent with the view that the moral value of the virtue, in so far as it manifests itself in our treatment of animals, derives from its connection with our treatment of human beings. Contracting rational agents should agree to try to develop a ready sympathy for one another's suffering, and sympathy for animal suffering is, on the current proposal, merely a side-effect of this general attitude.

I shall investigate in a later section just how powerful a constraint is placed on our treatment of animals by this account. But it seems plain, at least, that actions which cause suffering to animals will be wrong whenever they are performed for no reason, or for trivial reasons (on the grounds that they manifest brutish cruelty), or whenever they are performed for their own sake (since they will then manifest sadistic cruelty). So the hit-and-run driver to whom it never occurs to stop, in order to help the dog left howling in pain at the side of the road, as well as the one who drives on because late for an appointment at the hairdresser (as well as, of course, the driver who runs down the dog for fun in the first place), will each count as having acted wrongly, on the present account. For in each case the action will show the agent to be cruel.

Will this character-expressive account extend also to actions that cause the (painless) death of an animal? If so, then those who hunt animals for sport, or who kill them (or arrange to have them killed) for the pleasure of eating their flesh, will stand morally condemned. For if it were true that sympathy should be extended for the death of an animal as well as for its suffering, then it is plain that such actions would count as brutishly cruel, since the pleasures for which they are undertaken are trivial ones. In fact, however, it is doubtful whether we manifest cruelty by such killings, as I shall now try to explain.

It is obvious that beneficence towards human beings normally encompasses actions necessary to preserve life, as well as those necessary to prevent suffering. Thus callous Carl would surely constitute a paradigm of heartlessness, even if the process of drowning, undergone by the child he fails to rescue, were not itself a painful one. But this may only be so (at least in the first instance) where the life in question is the life of a rational agent. (Arguments similar to those deployed in Chapter 5 may then be used to widen the extent of the required attitude to include all human beings.) For recall that we are now viewing beneficence within the context of contractualism, and that rational contractors may be expected to value their own rational agency above all else. Moreover, recall from Chapter 3 that our reasons for fearing death derive from the fact that we have forward-looking desires that presuppose continued life. We would then expect rational contractors to agree to develop a general attachment to one another's lives. They will then be prepared, not only to avoid killing one another (a requirement of justice), but also to act positively to try to prevent death where possible, grounded in a sympathetic appreciation of the motives that rational agents have for going on living.

It counts in favour of the contractualist approach to these issues that when we enter sympathetically into the death of another, trying to see what their death may have meant from their point of view, we do seem naturally to focus on those plans and projects that have now been cut short. For this would explain the fact noted in Chapter 4, that many people feel less sympathy – from the perspective of the one who dies – for the death of a baby or an old person who has let go of their hold on life. For in such cases no forward-looking motives for survival may exist. But this sort of sympathy is only possible in respect of the death of a rational agent, since only such an agent has long-term projects, or the desire for continued life.

What emerges is this. The fact that the death of an animal may bring to an end a worthwhile existence and prevent future satisfactions of desire will acquire moral importance in the context of utilitarianism, but will lack such significance in the context of the present character-expressive account. That someone fails to be moved by the painless death of an animal need not display any cruelty. For there is no such thing, here, as entering sympathetically into the reasons that the animal had for going on living. Of course we could, if we wished, enter sympathetically into the future pleasures and satisfactions of the animal, which have now been lost through death. And no doubt if we were utilitarians we should be obliged to do so, as we saw in Chapter 4. But given that this is not what sympathy for the death of a rational agent normally amounts to, the fact that we fail to have such feelings in connection with the death of an animal need not show that there is anything amiss with our moral character.

REFLECTIVE EQUILIBRIUM ATTAINED

I believe that the account now sketched of our duties towards animals is sufficiently plausible to enable us to achieve reflective equilibrium overall. First, it can explain our common-sense belief that it is wrong to cause unnecessary suffering to an animal, where 'unnecessary' means either 'for no reason', 'for trivial reasons', or 'for its own sake'. (In the next section I shall consider what the implications of the account may be for practices that are more controversial, such as hunting, factory farming, and animal experimentation.) Second, the present approach also retains our intuitive belief that there can be no question of weighing animal suffering against the suffering of a human being. Since animals are still denied moral standing, on this contractualist account, they make no direct moral claims upon us. There is therefore nothing *to* be weighed against the claims of a human being. Finally, the account can retain the intuition shared by many people (including some champions of animals like Singer, as we saw in Chapter 4), that there need be nothing wrong with causing the painless death of an animal. Since the sort of sympathy that we should feel for the loss of a human life is only appropriate, in the first instance, in connection with the death of a rational agent, such actions may fail to manifest any degree of cruelty. (Some killings may, however, be *wasteful*, in the same sense that the motiveless cutting down of an oak tree may be.)

A further advantage of our account is that it can explain how people so easily come to be under the illusion, when they engage in theoretical reflection, that animal suffering has moral standing, mattering for its own sake. For those who have the right moral dispositions in this area will act for the sake of the animal when prompted by feelings of sympathy. Since right action requires that you act for the sake of the animal, it is then easy to see how one might slip into believing that the animal itself has moral standing. But this would be to miss the point that there may be a variety of different levels to moral thinking.[1] On the one hand there is the level of thought that manifests our settled moral dispositions and attitudes (this is where sympathy for animal suffering belongs), but on the other hand there is the level of theoretical reflection upon those dispositions and attitudes, asking how they may be justified by an acceptable moral theory. It is at this level that we come to realise, as contractualists, that animals are without moral standing.

For similar reasons, the proposed character-expressive account of our duties towards animals is able to avoid the charge of absurdity often levelled at Kant's somewhat similar treatment of the issue.[2] Kant is sometimes represented – unfairly – as claiming that those who perform acts of kindness towards animals are merely practising for kindness towards humans. As if anyone ever helped an animal with such an intention! But in fact he is best interpreted as presenting an account along the lines of that above, which distinguishes between the motives of those who act out of the sort of beneficent state of character they ought to have, and the theoretical explanation of the moral value that state possesses. It is only at the latter level that we may see the value of a sympathetic character as deriving from the way in which it manifests itself in our treatment of human beings.

It therefore looks as if the present proposal can account for every aspect of common sense. The only apparent difficulty remaining is that it denies that animal suffering has moral standing. However, this is not, properly, part of common sense itself, but is rather a theoretical construction upon it. Here the account can explain how we come to be under the illusion of direct significance. The contractualist treatment of animals thus has all the hallmarks of a powerful moral theory, acceptable under reflective equilibrium in the absence of any more plausible proposal. It remains to investigate the consequences of this approach for the controversial practices of hunting, factory farming, and laboratory experimentation upon animals.

CONTROVERSIAL CONSEQUENCES

How powerful a constraint does contractualism place on our behaviour towards animals, on the present account? That is to say, under what circumstances is it wrong to cause suffering to an animal, on the grounds that to do so would display cruelty or some other defect of character? Here our earlier observation becomes important, that whether or not a given act displays a defect may depend on the surrounding circumstances and the motive from which the action is performed. In the case where Astrid was adrift at sea, it was clear that no disrespect was shown to her grandfather by cutting up his corpse for bait. But it is worth noting that a similar act may be excusable when a great deal less than human life is at stake.

Suppose that Candy lives with her grandfather in a cabin in a particularly bleak part of Canada. For two months every winter they are completely snowed in, with drifts even covering the main windows. The only source of ventilation remaining is a small window under the eaves. Now suppose as before that the grandfather dies, and that, as is the way of all flesh, his body begins to decompose. In order to avoid the nauseating smell,

Candy cuts up his corpse into pieces small enough to throw out through the only functioning window. It seems to me that she no more lays herself open to criticism than did Astrid on her life-raft, although a great deal less than survival is at stake.

I think that all our judgements in such cases make substantial psychological assumptions, concerning what actions and attitudes are psychologically connected with, or separable from, others. We judge that Candy's action is permissible because we think that, taken together with its motives and circumstances, it may easily co-exist with a deep love of her grandfather, and with a respect for humanity of whatever strength we deem appropriate. In contrast, we think that lazy Jane's lack of preparedness to go to the aid of the man who collapses in front of her shows a lack of compassion that may manifest itself in other, more serious, circumstances.

When we apply these ideas to actions that cause suffering to animals, it turns out that almost any legitimate, non-trivial, motive is sufficient to make the action separable from a generally cruel or insensitive disposition. For example, consider technicians working in laboratories that use animals for the testing of detergents, causing them much suffering in the process. That they can become desensitised to animal suffering in such a context provides little reason for thinking that they will be any less sympathetic and generous persons outside it. Consider, also, farm-hands working in conditions that cause considerable suffering to the animals under their care. Again there seems no reason to think that they will thereby be more likely to be cruel or unsympathetic when it comes to dealing with other human beings in their society. Note that in both cases the motives from which the people in question are acting are by no means trivial, since they are earning a livelihood.

It is important to stress that the only basis for direct moral criticism of actions such as these that cause suffering to animals has to do with the qualities of character manifested by the individual actors. There is thus no scope, here, for criticising the overall practices of factory farming and animal experimentation. (We shall return in a later section to the argument from the legitimate concerns of animal lovers.) This point is important because even if the reasons why we have such practices are trivial – cheaper meat and new varieties of cosmetic – the motives of those who engage in them are not. There is then no reason to claim that those people are cruel in what they do.

It may be objected that a significant difference between Candy, the Canadian, and the laboratory technicians is that Candy's action is 'one off', whereas the actions of the technicians are continually being repeated. It may therefore be felt that, although the latter actions do not in themselves *display* a cruel character, they may be apt to *cause* such a character, through desensitisation to suffering, and may thus be morally condemned on that basis. But I think that human beings are more discriminating than this argument suggests. That someone can become desensitised to the suffering of an animal need not in any way mean that they have become similarly desensitised to the sufferings of human beings – the two things are, surely, psychologically separable.

Hunting may present a rather different case. For those who hunt animals for sport, rather than to feed themselves or to earn a living, do so from motives that must certainly count as trivial in comparison to the suffering they cause. While the pleasures of the hunt need not be directly sadistic – it need not be the suffering of the animal that is the object of enjoyment – they are inseparably bound up with the enjoyment of power, and of violent domination. (If the challenge of creeping up close to an animal through the woods were the only pleasure, then one could just as well hunt with a camera as a gun.) It does seem plausible that those who indulge such pleasures may be reinforcing aspects of their characters that may make them unfit, in various ways, for their moral dealings with human beings.

Part of the explanation for the psychological separability that I have claimed exists between attitudes to animal and human suffering lies in the obvious differences of physical form between animals and humans. Because most animals look and behave very differently from humans, it is easy to make and maintain a psychological distinction between one's attitudes to pain in the two cases. The most brutal butcher can, nevertheless, be the most loving parent and sympathetic friend. For this very reason, indeed, it seems to me (from a contractualist perspective, remember) to be a conventional, culturally determined, matter that one's attitudes towards animals should show anything at all about one's moral character, as I shall try to explain in the next section.

It may be objected that people's attitudes to the sufferings of different classes of human being are equally psychologically separable. White racists who are indifferent to the sufferings of blacks, for example, may nevertheless behave impeccably with respect to other whites. But this is not to the point. For such people are drawing distinctions amongst those who have moral standing, and who are therefore entitled to equal concern and consideration. The separability between attitudes to human and animal suffering, in contrast, is grounded in a distinction between those who have, and those who lack, moral standing. There is therefore no direct moral objection to those who are able to keep their attitudes to pain separate in the two cases.

ANIMALS AND CULTURE

There are a number of different respects in which our particular form of society encourages a connection between our attitudes towards animals, on the one hand, and human beings on the other. The first is that many of us keep animals as pets. Now people do keep some strange pets, including alligators, spiders, and stick-insects. But in general they keep the sorts of animals that are most human, particularly in their response to affection. In fact, we model our relationships with our pets on our relations with other human beings, and these relationships serve many of the same purposes of companionship and the enjoyment of shared experience. Since we treat pets as honorary humans, as it were, it follows that if someone can be cruel to a pet then this is fairly direct evidence of a generally cruel disposition.

The second point about our society, a correlative of the first, is that for most of us our *only* direct contact with animals is with pets. This is largely a product of increasing urbanisation. It also makes contemporary Western culture unique in all human history. In all other cultures the majority of people would also have had extensive contact with animals in the course of their work, whether hunting, farming, or through other forms of labour such as towing barges and lifting weights. It cannot be an accident that our society has, in consequence, recently seen an explosion of sentimentality towards animals.

The final point about our society is that we frequently use animals as moral exemplars in the training of the young. (This may be connected with a phenomenon we noted in Chapter 6 – namely, the extent of anthropomorphism now present in children's literature.) It may be true of many children in our society that their first introduction to moral notions is to be told that it is cruel to pull the whiskers out of the cat. So, again, if someone is cruel to an animal, then this is evidence that something may have gone drastically wrong with their moral education.

These features of our society are highly contingent. There may be (indeed, there are) many other societies in which animals are not accorded these roles. In such a society a dog may be slowly strangled to death because this is believed to make the meat taste better, while it never occurs to the people involved that there is any connection between what they are doing and their attitudes to human beings – indeed, there may in fact be no such connection. While such an action performed by someone in our society would manifest cruelty, when done by them it may not.

It therefore seems to me that, while contractualism can find a place for the indirect moral significance of animals, and for duties towards them, it is a fairly minimal and culturally determined place. Given certain facts about our society, it may be true that some behaviour towards animals is wrong because of what is shown about the character of the agent. But what is shown may not be very much, in many circumstances. And there may be other social conditions in which nothing of moral significance would be shown at all. While contractualism is thus vindicated, in that it can explain how there is a large element of truth in our common-sense attitudes towards animals, at the same time little or no comfort is given to those who would wish to extend greater moral protection to animals.

One question remains at this point: to what extent is the role of animals in our particular society morally desirable? That people need pets at all is, arguably, a product of the social alienation felt by many people in societies as fluid and fragmentary as ours, and we could surely engage in successful moral education of the young without using animals as exemplars. We therefore need to look at the question whether current attitudes towards animals may not be getting in the way of other, more fundamental, moral concerns. I shall return to this issue in the final section of the chapter.

NON-RATIONAL HUMANS RE-VISITED

The position reached above, concerning the limitations of our obligations towards animals, would of course carry little conviction if contractualists were forced to say similar things about our treatment of those human beings who are not rational agents – namely, young babies, severe mental defectives, and the very senile. For no one is going to accept that babies may be factory farmed for their meat, or that aggressive mental defectives may be killed in the way that one might put down a vicious dog. Now in the final sections of Chapter 5 I presented arguments from the danger of a slippery slope, and from social stability, for the conclusion that all categories of human being should be accorded the same basic direct rights. Those arguments can now be strengthened by points arising from our present discussion of attitudes to suffering.

No doubt human babies, mental defectives, and senile old people may enjoy similar levels of mental activity to animals – frequently lower, in fact. But in other respects they will have a moral salience that is quite different from that of animals. The crucial point is that they share human form, and many human patterns of behaviour, with those who are rational agents. It is no mere accident of culture or upbringing that a crying baby, or a senile old woman moaning with the pain of terminal cancer, can evoke our sympathy. For what is presented to our senses in these cases differs only in slight degree from the suffering of a child or normal adult. We should therefore expect sensitivity to the one form of suffering to be closely psychologically connected with sensitivity to the sufferings of those human beings who are rational agents. Someone who behaves in such a way as to be indifferent to the suffering of a baby or a senile old lady is therefore very wrong, because of what their behaviour reveals about their character, quite apart from any question of infringements of rights. That they can act in such a way is almost certain to manifest cruelty.

This is not to say, of course, that we need be psychologically incapable of drawing distinctions within the category of human beings, and of arranging our moral attitudes accordingly. On the contrary, it is plain that many people in the course of human history have done just this. Some of these distinctions, for example on racial or sexual grounds, mark divisions within the class of rational agents, and may therefore be directly condemned on grounds of justice. But the general point is that it is highly dangerous to attempt to draw distinctions within the category of human beings at all. Given the immense similarities of appearance and behaviour that exist amongst all human beings, whatever their intellectual status, attempts to ground attitudes to suffering on distinctions between them are likely to undermine attitudes to suffering elsewhere. Those who begin by rationalising their indifference to the sufferings of the senile may end by so warping their attitudes and moral imagination that they become insensitive to the sufferings of some who are, indisputably, rational agents.

Rational contractors who are trying to agree on the rules that will assign basic rights and duties should therefore be aware that any attempt to draw distinctions within the category of human beings may have psychological effects that would prove morally disastrous. They should then agree to assign basic moral rights to all human beings, irrespective of their status as rational agents. For suppose that they were to agree on a rule excluding mental defectives from possessing moral standing, and were thus to allow that there is no direct moral objection to killing or hurting such a being. This rule would clash powerfully with our natural impulse of sympathy for the sufferings of all who share human form, and may cause the latter to be undermined. If so, then our duties towards rational agents would also be endangered.

In contrast, no similar dangers attend the exclusion of animals from possession of moral standing. (Nor, arguably, are there such dangers in the exclusion of human foetuses, in their early stages of development. So abortion may remain a moral option.) For there is a large gulf, both of physical form and modes of behaviour, between human beings and even their closest animal cousins. A dividing line drawn here, being clear-cut, and appealing to features that are strikingly salient, may therefore be a stable one. For it will then be easy to create and maintain a psychological distinction between one's attitude towards suffering in the two cases.

INDIRECT ARGUMENTS AGAIN

Let us review our conclusions thus far. Since animals are not rational agents, they will not, in the first instance at least, be accorded direct moral rights under contractualism. But then nor are there slippery slope or social stability arguments for granting them such rights. Animals have indirect moral significance nevertheless, in virtue of the qualities of moral character they may evoke in us. Actions involving animals that are expressive of a bad moral character are thereby wrong. Because attitudes to animal and human suffering may be readily psychologically separated, however, the constraints so far placed on our treatment of animals are minimal ones. All that follows is that it is wrong (in our culture) to cause suffering to an animal for trivial reasons, or to obtain sadistic pleasure.

It seems that nothing bad need be displayed in the moral character of someone whose job involves testing detergents on animals, or in farm-hands whose practices cause suffering to the animals under their care (provided, at least, that they try to minimise the pain that they cause, in so far as this can be done without great cost to themselves). Nor need there be anything amiss with the characters of those who employ such people, since their motive will generally be to retain the profitability and competitiveness of their business, which is certainly not trivial. So in all such cases, there is neither a direct moral objection (no rights are infringed), nor is there any indirect moral objection arising out of a judgement on the character of the agent. Even in the case of activities, such as hunting, where there is a moral objection on grounds of character, it would hardly be permissible to intervene, as do hunt saboteurs. For we do not think it right, in general, that we should try to force people to change their characters, in advance of them performing actions that constitute infringements of right. For example, even if there were reliable psychological tests for aggressiveness, we surely would not think it right that those who score highly in such tests should be required to undergo treatment, in advance of evidence of actual violent behaviour towards others.

There remains, however, the question of the likely offence to animal lovers, discussed in Chapter 5. While this was rejected at the time as an adequate basis on which to ground all moral duties towards animals, it might still be re-introduced, at this point, as an argument for forbidding hunting, factory farming, and many forms of animal experimentation. For it now emerges that there is a major difference between this sort of offence, and the offence caused to prudish people by the thought of unusual sexual practices. This is because distress at the thought of an animal suffering is a response that we may want people to have, if the argument of this chapter has been sound. It is a response that both manifests and reinforces an admirably sympathetic character. Sexual prudery, in contrast, has no particular moral worth. So while the retort 'If it upsets you, don't think about it' may be appropriate for the latter group, it is not appropriate for the former. The concern of animal lovers for the sufferings of animals is not only legitimate, but expressive of a morally admirable state of character. We may wonder, then, whether this is sufficient to render such practices as hunting and factory farming morally unacceptable – not because of any infringement of animal rights, but because those practices are insufficiently respectful of the concerns of animal lovers.

Some might be puzzled at how I can claim, on the one hand, that sympathy for animal suffering is expressive of an admirable state of character and yet claim, on the other, that those who become desensitised to such suffering in the course of their work need not thereby display any weakness in their character. How can I have it both ways? The answer is that the contexts are different in the two cases. Those who become distressed when they think of the animals suffering in our factory farms and experimental laboratories do so, as it were, in the abstract – in independence from any further morally significant purpose. Those who become desensitised to that very same suffering, on the other hand, do so in the context of earning a living. Roughly speaking, the position to emerge from this chapter is that sensitivity to animal suffering is admirable when, and only when, it fails to interfere with purposes that are morally significant in a more direct sense.

But now we have a difficulty. For the proposal that factory farming and animal experimentation should be forbidden because they encroach on the sensibilities of animal lovers, means that those feelings *would* be interfering with morally significant purposes, namely the purposes of earning a living and of maintaining a viable business. In this case it would seem that the latter must take priority. It is too much to demand that people should forgo employment out of respect for the feelings of animal lovers, just as it is too much to demand that the owner of an ancient building should do without a habitable residence out of respect for the feelings of those who would not wish to see the building altered. If the legitimate feelings of animal lovers are to have any important place in this debate, it will not be as a ground for criticising the individual practitioners, but rather as a basis for criticism of the practice as a whole. What might be claimed is that, out of respect for these feelings, the organisation of our society should be altered so that it has no need for practices that cause suffering to animals on a regular basis – where the changes should include compensation for those who might lose employment or income as a result.

We are now brought back to the question of public policy we left open earlier – namely, whether we want to encourage and reinforce the psychological connection that already exists, in our culture, between attitudes to animal and human suffering. Or is this connection already too strong, so that there is a moral case for trying to weaken it? As we noted earlier, there are forces in our culture that are responsible for this connection, and arguably these forces are increasing. With increasing wealth, and yet increasing social alienation, more and more people are keeping pets. And young children are increasingly exposed to forms of entertainment in which anthropomorphic treatments of animals are rife. Yet there are no particular moral gains in this tendency. On the contrary. To restrict current patterns of treatment of animals out of respect for the sensibilities of animal lovers would only reinforce a trend that has considerable moral costs.

There would be economic and social costs of placing further restrictions on our treatment of animals, particularly if factory farming and scientific experiments on animals were forbidden. But I do not wish to focus especially on these. More important is that the cost of increasing concern with animal welfare is to distract attention from the needs of those who certainly do have moral standing – namely, human beings. We live on a planet where millions of our fellow humans starve, or are near starving, and where many millions more are undernourished. In addition, the twin perils of pollution and exhaustion of natural resources threaten the futures of ourselves and our descendants. It is here that moral attention should be focussed. Concern with animal welfare, while expressive of states of character that are admirable, is an irrelevance to be opposed rather than encouraged. Our response to animal lovers should not be 'If it upsets you, don't think about it', but rather 'If it upsets you, think about something more important'.

It may be objected that it is always possible to think about *both*. It might be claimed, indeed, that increased concern for animals will help to foster the attitudes of general sympathy and respect for the environment that will be necessary in tackling the world's wider problems. But in fact, much of the moral energy currently spent in defence of animals has been diverted from other domains. Amongst those who campaign actively on behalf of animals, indeed, the feelings of sympathy that motivate their actions have ceased to be morally admirable, precisely because those feelings have been allowed to get in the way of concerns that are more directly morally significant. Moreover, there is no way in which we can, as contractualists, tell ourselves a plausible story in which increased concern for animals will be morally beneficial. For we ought to be able to see clearly that it is only the sufferings of humans that have moral standing, and that have direct moral significance irrespective of facts about character. In which case, increased feelings of sympathy for animals can only serve to undermine our judgements of relative importance, having the same moral effect as *de*creased concern for humans. So if contractualism provides us with the best framework for moral theory, as I have argued that it does, then we should wish to roll back the tide of current popular concern with animal welfare.

SUMMARY

Contractualism withholds direct moral rights from animals, while at the same time granting them to all human beings. Yet contractualism can explain our common-sense belief that animals should not be caused to suffer for trivial reasons, since causing such suffering is expressive of a cruel character. This position is sufficiently plausible to be acceptable under reflective equilibrium. But the constraints thus justified are minimal. Contractualism certainly provides no support for those who would wish to extend still further the moral protection already available to animals.

CHAPTER 8

Animals and conscious experience

In this chapter I shall explore a challenge to something we have taken for granted throughout our investigation of the moral standing of animals, at least since Chapter 3. The assumption in question is that animal experiences (particularly pain) are sufficiently similar to our own to be appropriate objects of moral concern.

CONSCIOUS VERSUS NON-CONSCIOUS

I shall begin by drawing a distinction between two different kinds of mental state, that is particularly vivid in the case of experience. While not exactly a common-sense distinction, it is easily recognised when pointed out. Consider some familiar examples. Suppose that Abbie is driving her car over a route she knows well, her conscious attention wholly abstracted from her surroundings. Perhaps she is thinking deeply about some aspect of her work, or fantasising about her next summer holiday, to the extent of being unaware of what she is doing on the road. Suddenly she 'comes to', returning her attention to the task in hand with a startled realisation that she has not the faintest idea what she has been doing or seeing for some minutes past. Yet there is a clear sense in which she must have been seeing, or she would have crashed the car. Her passenger sitting next to her may correctly report that she had seen a vehicle double-parked by the side of the road, for example, since she deftly steered the car around it. But she was not aware of seeing that obstacle, either at the time or later in memory.

Another example: when washing up dishes I generally put on music to help pass the time. If it is a piece that I love particularly well I may become totally absorbed, ceasing to be conscious of what I am doing at the sink. Yet someone observing me position a glass neatly on the rack to dry between two coffee mugs would correctly say that I must have seen that those mugs were already there, or I should not have placed the glass where I did. Yet I was not aware of seeing those mugs, or of placing the glass between them. At the time I was swept up in the Finale of Schubert's *Arpeggione Sonata*, and if asked even a moment later I should not have been able to recall what I had been looking at.

Let us call such experiences *non-conscious* ones. What does it feel like to be the subject of a non-conscious experience? It feels like nothing. It does not feel like anything to have a non-conscious visual experience as of a vehicle parked at the side of the road, or as of two coffee mugs placed on a draining rack – precisely because to have such an experience is not to be conscious of it. Only conscious experiences have a distinctive phenomenology, a distinctive feel. Non-conscious experiences are ones that may help to control behaviour without being felt by the conscious subject.

Intuitive as these points are, they are already sufficient to show that it is wrong to identify the question whether a creature has experiences with the question whether there is something that it feels like to be that thing.[1] For there is a class – perhaps a large class – of non-conscious experiences that have no phenomenology. So the fact that a creature has sense-organs, and can be observed to display in its behaviour sensitivity to the salient features of its surrounding environment, is insufficient to establish that it feels like anything to be that thing. It may be that the experiences of animals are wholly of the non-conscious variety. It is an open question whether there is anything that it feels like to be a bat, or a dog, or a monkey. If consciousness is like the turning on of a light, then it may be that their lives are nothing but darkness. In order to make progress with this issue, we need to understand the nature of the distinction between conscious and non-conscious mental states.

Before proceeding to that task, however, it is worth noticing a somewhat less familiar example of non-conscious experience, since this will help us to see how the distinction between conscious and non-conscious states may have a physical realisation in the neurological structure of the human brain. It will also help us to rebut a possible objection to the examples so far considered, that the phenomenon they exhibit is one of instantaneous memory loss, rather than lack of conscious awareness. The example I have in mind is that of blindsight. Human subjects who have suffered lesions in the striate cortex (the visual centre in the higher part of the brain) may lose all conscious experience in an area of their visual field. They insist that they can see nothing at all within that region. Nevertheless, if asked to guess, they prove remarkably good at describing features of objects presented to them in that area, such as the orientation of a line, or at pointing out the direction of a light-source.[2] Subjects can also reach out and grasp objects of varying shapes and sizes, at various distances, with about 80–90 per cent of normal accuracy. Indeed, if asked to catch a ball thrown towards them from their blind side they often prove successful.[3]

The conclusion to be drawn from these studies is that while blindsight patients lack conscious visual experience within an area of their visual field, they nevertheless have non-conscious experiences that are somehow made available to help in the control of their actions. It seems that the neurological explanation for the phenomenon is that information from the eye is not only mapped onto the striate cortex (in normal subjects), but is also sent to a second mapping in the midbrain. It is presumably this latter mapping that is made available, in blindsight patients, to be integrated with the subject's goals and other perceptions in controlling behaviour. It is also possible that it is this midbrain information that underlies the everyday examples of non-conscious experience outlined earlier. But we should beware of concluding that any creature with a striate cortex will be the subject of conscious visual experiences. The phenomenon of blindsight shows only that a functioning striate cortex is a physically necessary condition for conscious visual experience, not that it is sufficient. It may be that in the case of everyday non-conscious experience the striate cortex is indeed active, but that its information is not made available to whatever structures in the human brain underlie consciousness. And it may be that even animals with a striate cortex do not possess those structures at all.

It is worth stressing that the various non-conscious experiences we have been considering do genuinely deserve to be counted as kinds of experience. For not only is in-coming information processed to quite a high degree of sophistication, but the states in question conform to the practical-reasoning-model of explanation. Thus Abbie, the absent-minded driver, behaved as she did because she *wanted* to reach her destination safely and *saw* that the vehicle was an obstacle in her path. And blindsight patients may pick up a ball because they *want* to comply with the request of the experimenter and *see* that the ball is on the edge of the desk. But if someone really insists that experiences are conscious states as a matter of definition, then the conclusion of this section may simply be re-phrased. It is that since there exist in humans similar levels of cognitive processing and behaviour control to those displayed by animals, which do not involve experiences, it is an open question whether animals have experiences at all. However, in the discussion that follows I shall assume, as seems most natural, that not all experiences are conscious ones.

The distinction drawn here between two types of experience is probably quite general, applying to all categories of mental state. But to see how it applies in the case of beliefs and desires we need to draw a further distinction, between a belief or desire that is *activated* (engaged in current mental processes) and one that is *dormant* (possessed, but not currently being used). Most of our beliefs and desires lie dormant for most of the time. I continue to have beliefs about my parents' birthdays, for example, throughout both my waking and sleeping life. But only occasionally do these beliefs become activated, as when I fill out a passport renewal form and have to complete a section headed 'Dates of birth of parents'.

It seems highly likely that beliefs and desires can become activated without becoming conscious. When I play chess, for example, I rely on my knowledge of the rules of the game, but without that knowledge normally surfacing in consciousness. My beliefs about the rules of chess become activated, helping to control my thoughts and my actions, but without becoming conscious. Similarly, in the example of Abbie, the absent-minded driver, Abbie's desire to avoid obstacles will be activated without becoming conscious. So in connection with activated beliefs and desires, at least, we can certainly draw a distinction between those that are conscious and those that are non-conscious.

While the activation of beliefs and desires in these examples is non-conscious, the dormant states themselves will normally remain available to consciousness – I can recall the rules of chess if I wish, and on reflection Abbie will avow her desire to avoid a crash. But there may also be cases in which beliefs or desires can help to control behaviour without being accessible to the conscious subject at all. For example, if Freudian theories of the mind are anywhere near correct, then this will be true of the beliefs and desires that Freudians characterise as *un*conscious.

CARTESIAN CONSCIOUSNESS

Having drawn an intuitive distinction between conscious and non-conscious mental states, our next task must be to give an account of the nature of that distinction. One popular answer, following in the tradition of Descartes, would equate con-sciousness with subjective, qualitative, feel. On this account, a conscious mental state is one with a distinctive phenomenology, and a non-conscious mental state is one without. This will not do, however. While it may look plausible in connection with the distinction between conscious and non-conscious experience, it cannot be applied to the distinction between conscious and non-conscious belief or desire. Entertaining a conscious belief in one's mother's birthday does not feel like anything. Conscious activations of belief and desire are not introspectively recognised in virtue of their distinctive subjective character, in the way that conscious pains and tickles arguably are, since such events have no phenomenology. So whatever it is that makes a conscious belief to be conscious, it cannot be the way it feels. Yet as conscious beliefs do not seem to be conscious in a different *sense* from conscious experiences, we need to provide a unitary account to cover the two cases, if we can.

The assimilation of consciousness to qualitative feel might be defended against these points by means of an argument containing three steps. First, it might be claimed that activations of belief and desire become conscious by virtue of emerging in conscious acts of thinking. Second, it may be said that conscious thinkings consist, in one way or another, of images, or mental pictures. Then thirdly, it might be claimed that conscious images *are* conscious by virtue of their distinctive feels, just as conscious experiences are. I have no quarrel with the first premiss of this argument, and, suitably interpreted, I might be prepared to accept the second (I shall comment on this later). But the third premiss is definitely wrong. It is false that mental images are conscious, and recognisable as such, by virtue of their distinctive phenomenology. In which case the attempt to equate consciousness with possession of a subjective feel fails.

The crucial point is that mental images are not made up of experiences. For all experiences must occur within some sensation field. All visual experiences, for example, must occur in the visual field, standing in (perceived) spatial relationships with all other visual experiences enjoyed at the same time. But mental images, of a given type (auditory, visual, and so on), do not occur within the sensation fields of the corresponding type, as one would expect if mental images consisted of sensations having a distinctive subjective feel. My argument for this is that mental images do not interfere with normal perception in the way that after-images, for example, do.

The point here needs stating with some care. For what is true is that mental images, of a given type, will interfere with mental tasks involving experiences of the same type.[4] Being asked to form a visual image of a particular word, for example, will interfere with visual recognition tasks, but not those requiring auditory recognition. So it is clear that visual imagery must utilise some of the same cognitive resources as does visual perception. But this does not show that visual images consist of visual sensations, and thus have a distinctive phenomenology. The contrast between mental images and after-images will make this clear. When I look away from a bright light at a plain wall and experience a red after-image, the wall itself looks red in consequence. But when I imagine a red tomato while looking at a white wall, the wall does *not* look red. While mental imaging may utilise some of the same cognitive resources as does perception, it does not compete with it phenomenologically.

The truth is that imaging is an intellectual activity, not a kind of experience. When we form a mental image of something we represent to ourselves how that thing would appear to us in some sense-modality. In this we are active, not passive. Our introspective awareness of our own current acts of imagination is not to be assimilated to awareness of subjective feel. What makes a conscious image conscious is not the way it feels. For, unlike the experiences that they represent, images do not in fact have an immediate qualitative feel. Quite what does, then, explain their status as conscious is something I shall return to later.

OTHER THEORIES OF CONSCIOUSNESS

If the attempt to assimilate consciousness to subjective feel fails, how else might one try to account for the distinction between conscious and non-conscious mental states? There are a number of obviously inadequate suggestions. First, it might be said that the distinctive feature of a conscious experience is that it is recorded in short-term memory. This would be the reason why, in the case of Abbie, the absent-minded driver, there is no memory of experience even a moment later. But this suggestion is implausible, since there is nothing here to distinguish conscious from non-conscious short-term memory. Yet there seems no reason why there cannot be such a thing as non-conscious short-term memory. On the contrary, one would expect that there might be many different areas of cognition where a brief record of events is held.

Second, it might be said that a conscious state is one that is available to the organism as a whole. But the trouble here is that the experiences of any earthworm or slug will turn out to be conscious ones, on this account, whereas the experiences of Abbie, the absent-minded driver, are not. Besides, there will be severe problems in defining what it means for a state to be available to the whole organism. For there may be many regions of cognition to which the content of a conscious experience is not made available, just as there are regions of cognition (that is, those that involve consciousness) to which non-conscious experiences are not made available. There seems no good theoretical reason why the former should be counted as being available to the whole organism, while the latter should not.

A development of this second suggestion might be to claim that conscious states are those that are available to an organism's main decision-making processes.[5] This avoids the problem of explaining what it means for an experience to be available to the organism as a whole. But it still faces the difficulty that the experiences of an earthworm will count as conscious, on this proposal, (provided that earthworms have decision-making processes) whereas Abbie's will not – despite the fact that her experiences are engaged in processes of decision making that are considerably more complex and varied, and much more conceptually sophisticated, than those of the earthworm. Moreover, it is left extremely puzzling, on this account, why the mere fact of height in a hierarchy of control should be thought sufficient to make the difference between conscious and non-conscious status. Suppose, for example, that it is possible for my main decision-making processes to be destroyed by brain damage, while leaving the rest of my cognition functioning normally. So I may still be able to drive a car, walk around without tripping over obstacles, and otherwise engage in those semi-automatic activities that do not usually require conscious attention. Suppose also, that for some time before this accident I had been blindsighted in a region of my visual field. Will it not follow, on the above account, that after my accident my blindsight experiences are suddenly conscious ones – because they are available to what would then be my *main* decision-making processes? But this seems intuitively absurd.[6]

A much more plausible, and popular, suggestion is the one first put forward by David Armstrong.[7] This characterises conscious mental states as those that give rise (non-inferentially) to an activated second-order belief in their own existence. Thus a conscious belief that such-and-such is one that, besides being available to enter into the causation of the subject's behaviour, is apt to cause in them the activated belief that they believe that such-and-such. Similarly, a conscious visual experience is one that, besides causing beliefs about the matter to which the experience relates and being made available to non-conscious motor control processes, is apt to give rise to the belief that just such an experience is taking place.

If such an account were correct, then it would be very doubtful whether many species of animal could be said to enjoy conscious experiences. For as we saw in Chapter 6, there is no reason to justify attributing second-order beliefs to most species of mammal. The only exceptions we allowed were the great apes, particularly chimpanzees. I shall argue that the proposed account is definitely incorrect, however. But this result is not a defence of conscious experience for animals. Quite the contrary – the account of consciousness that emerges will make it even less likely that any animals have conscious experiences.

I begin with an example designed to show that one cannot equate conscious believing that such-and-such with an aptness to cause activated second-order beliefs that one believes that such-and-such. In the course of a discussion of the merits and demerits of contractualism, I might realise that I had for some time been speaking of contractualists as 'we', also becoming angry when their views were maligned – thus manifesting the activated second-order belief that I believe myself to believe in contractualism. But this might strike me with the force of self-discovery. If anyone had asked me previously whether I was a contractualist, I might have expressed uncertainty. In which case it would seem that the possession of activated second-order beliefs is not sufficient for conscious believing.

Another argument with the same conclusion is that the proposed account gets the content of conscious believing quite wrong (or rather, it misdescribes the contents of my mind when I entertain a conscious belief). For conscious believing is surely world-directed in precisely the way that belief itself is. If I entertain the conscious belief that the earth is getting warmer, then the *only* object of my (activated) belief may be the earth and its likely future temperature. Indeed, both the belief and the conscious belief surely possess the very same content. Whereas if the proposed account were correct, then in possessing the conscious belief I should also, and at the same time, possess a belief whose object would be myself (I should be believing of myself that I possess a particular first-order belief). This just does not seem true to the phenomenon of conscious believing.

This point holds also for the proposed account of the distinction between conscious and non-conscious experience. Conscious visual experiences, too, are primarily world-directed. When I consciously see that there is a dagger on the desk before me, the primary (often the only) focus of my attention is the dagger itself. In normal cases of conscious perception our experiences are, as it were, transparent – representing the world to us without themselves being objects of attention. It is, of course, possible to pay attention to one's conscious experiences, as when I attempt a phenomenological description of my visual field. But this is a sophisticated and relatively unusual thing to do. Whereas on the proposed account it is the normal case – to perceive consciously that there is a dagger on the desk would be to have activated the belief about myself that I have an experience of there being a dagger on the desk.

Daniel Dennett has proposed a theory of consciousness that looks more promising, in some respects.[8] He maintains that conscious experiences are those that are held in a special short-term memory store whose function is to make them available to a speech production, or language, unit. Roughly, conscious experiences are those that are available for the subject to *report*. This gives the right sort of content to conscious experience, since the reports will generally be reports of what my experiences are *of* – for example, that there is a dagger on the desk. It also explains the examples with which we began, since neither Abbie, the absent-minded driver, nor someone who is blind-sighted, will have any disposition to make reports about their environment on the basis of their experiences. However, the account cannot easily be extended to cover the conscious status of conscious beliefs and desires. It also seems implausible in tying the phenomena of consciousness so closely to the capacity to speak a language. For example, we would surely want to say that the intelligent Martians discussed in Chapter 6 might have conscious experiences and thoughts. Yet, in lacking a natural language, they would lack any disposition to make reports on their states.

CONSCIOUSNESS AND CONSCIOUS THINKING

Is it possible to do better? Indeed it is. We can develop Dennett's model in such a way that consciousness is defined, not by its relation to speech production, but rather by its relation to a faculty of thinking, in which occurrent thoughts are regularly made available to be thought about in their turn. In fact, I propose that a conscious, as opposed to a non-conscious, mental state is one that is available to conscious thought – where a conscious act of thinking is itself an event that is available to be thought about similarly in turn. (When we think things consciously to ourselves, the events that express our thoughts are themselves regularly made available to be objects of further thoughts – I can think to myself that my thought was poorly formulated, or hasty, or confused, or whatever.) Although there is a hint of circularity in this suggestion, it is not in fact so. Rather, the account is reflexive. It is the very same thing that makes thinking conscious as makes experience or belief conscious – namely, availability to thought that is, in turn, regularly made available to thought.

In the case of belief, I propose that a conscious belief (*qua* dormant state) is one that is apt to emerge in a conscious thinking with the same content. This is then able to handle our earlier example in which I believe myself to believe in contractualism without consciously entertaining any such belief. The reason why I had not consciously believed contractualism to be true is that I failed to have any disposition to think to myself 'Contractualism is true'. The account also has the advantage that conscious beliefs have the same primary world-directedness as beliefs. For the conscious act of thinking, aptness to emerge in which is the distinctive mark of a conscious belief, is an event with the very same (world-directed) content as that belief itself. What makes my belief that the earth is getting warmer a conscious one is that I am disposed in suitable circumstances to think to myself 'The earth is getting warmer'. In both cases the direction of focus is on the world alone, rather than on myself.

In the case of experience, I propose that a conscious experience is a state whose existence and content are available to be consciously thought about (that is, available for description in acts of thinking that are themselves made available to further acts of thinking). In this case I say 'available to be thought *about*', rather than 'apt to emerge in thinkings with the same content', because it is plausible that most experiences have a degree of richness and complexity that can outreach our powers of description. Nevertheless, every aspect of the perceived scene is made available to thought, even if only the thought that things are now subtly different. (While the manner in which the leaves of a tree are shimmering in the breeze may defy description, I must at least be able to think to myself that the pattern of movement is now slightly altered, if it is.) Here, too, we can retain the primary world-directedness of conscious experience, since the normal way for information that is made available to thought through perception to emerge in acts of thinking, is in thoughts about the object perceived – as when I think to myself that the dagger on the desk is richly ornamented.

When we turn to consider, not conscious experience of something in the world, but the more sophisticated state of consciousness of the properties of that conscious experience itself, it is important to note that the suggested account is consistent with the existence of qualitative feelings whose distinctive nature is unanalysable. It may indeed be the case, as many maintain, that the distinctive feel of my experience of a warm shade of red is incapable of further analysis, or even of non-relational description. But I claim that what constitutes that feeling as a conscious rather than a non-conscious state, is that it is available to be consciously thought about. It is the status of subjective feelings as conscious states that is being analysed on the proposed account, not the individual feelings themselves.

While we can in principle distinguish a conscious experience, such as consciously seeing that there is a dagger on the desk, from the consciousness that one has such an experience, it could plausibly be maintained that the possibility of the latter is a necessary condition for the former. That is, we can hold that an experience will only count as conscious, and possess a distinctive phenomenal feel, if it is present to a faculty of thinking that is capable of distinguishing between experiences as such. There will only be something that my experiences *are like*, for me, if I am capable of drawing distinctions and making comparisons between them.[9] But note that this is not to say that I need actually make such comparisons in the normal case.

Notice that my proposal will extend quite naturally to explain the status, as conscious, of conscious mental images. What makes acts of imaging conscious, when they are, is that they are in turn made available to be consciously thought about – one can think about what one has imaged, and how. Note also that this explanation remains the same even if thinkings themselves consist of images, as some have maintained. (In its most plausible version, the claim would be that thinkings consist, at least partly, of imaged conversations, or of imaged acts of speech.) For as we pointed out earlier, to say that an act of thinking is conscious is to say that it is in turn made available to conscious thought.

Besides the virtues mentioned above, my account provides a natural treatment of the examples of non-conscious experience with which we began. The reason why Abbie's perception of the double-parked vehicle was not conscious, is that while information about the vehicle was somehow made available for integration into her actions, it was not available to her conscious thoughts. Similarly, in the example of non-conscious perception of mugs on a draining-board what made the experience non-conscious is that there was, in the circumstances, nothing available for me to think spontaneously about those mugs.

The issue of spontaneity is important in handling the

blindsight examples. For although in these cases the visual information is, in a sense, available to be thought about (since if asked to guess what is there, subjects will generally guess correctly), it is not apt to give rise to spontaneous thoughts in the way that conscious experiences are. In the normal course of events the blindsighted person will have no thoughts whatever about objects positioned in the blind portion of their visual field. Indeed, when they do think about the matter they are strongly inclined to believe that they see nothing. We can explain this within the theory. For what constitutes an experience as conscious, on my account, is that it is contained in a special short-term memory store that is *defined by its function* in making perceptual information immediately available to a faculty of reflexive thinking. This leaves open the possibility that perceptual information may sometimes be made available to thinking by other routes, as is presumably the case in connection with blindsight.

One final virtue of my account is that it is able to explain why so many philosophers, including Dennett, have been inclined to connect possession of conscious mental states with the ability to speak a natural language. For such a connection is at its most plausible (although still denied by many) where conscious thinkings are concerned. The idea that the ability to think things consciously to oneself is tied to the possession of a natural language has an immediate (if defeasible) plausibility. Whereas a similar thesis applied to the capacity for conscious experience may seem much more puzzling. For why should it be supposed that language-mastery is a necessary condition for a creature to enjoy conscious visual experiences? If the account sketched above is correct, there may indeed be such a connection, but at one remove – it is because conscious experiences are those that are available to conscious thinkings. Now although I am in fact one of those who maintain that language-mastery is at least contingently connected with the capacity for conscious thought, I shall not argue for this here.[10]

ANIMAL CONSCIOUSNESS

Animals are, of course, often conscious, in the sense that they are aware of the world around them and of the states of their own bodies. Animals can be awake, asleep, dreaming, comatose, or partly conscious, just as we can. They can be conscious, or fail to be conscious, of an acrid smell, a loud noise, or a shove from behind, just as we can. These facts are not at issue. I argued in Chapters 3 and 6 that all mammals, at least, have beliefs, desires, and sensations, and nothing that I say here is intended to challenge that. Granted that animals can be conscious *of* events, our question is whether those states of awareness are, themselves, conscious ones. Our question is not, whether animals have mental states, but whether animals are subject to *conscious* mental states.

If my account of the distinction between conscious and non-conscious mental states may be taken as established, then the non-conscious status of most animal experiences follows with very little further argument. For if it is implausible to ascribe second-order beliefs to birds, mice, or dogs, it is even more unlikely that such creatures might be thinking things consciously to themselves – that is to say, that they should engage in acts of thinking that are themselves regularly made available for the organism to think about. I assume that no one would seriously maintain that dogs, cats, sheep, cattle, pigs, or chickens consciously think things to themselves (let alone that fish or reptiles do). In which case, if my account of the distinction between conscious and non-conscious experience is correct, the experiences of all these creatures will be of the non-conscious variety.

What of the higher primates, however? We agreed in Chapter 6 that chimpanzees, at least, have second-order beliefs. Might it be plausible to ascribe to them conscious thinkings about their own thoughts as well? Well first, it might be questioned whether anything quite this strong is needed. For why should consciousness require availability to *conscious* thought? Why would not mere availability to thought do? One reply is that it would be very puzzling indeed how states could be conscious in virtue with their connection with states that are *not* conscious. (As if a surface could be illuminated by darkness!) Another reply parallels the point made earlier, in criticism of the suggestion that consciousness be equated with short-term memory. It is that there might be a number of different regions of cognition where information is made available to thought, or something like thought, without, intuitively, thereby becoming conscious. In the case of Abbie, the absent-minded driver, for example, the perception of a double-parked vehicle was presumably made available to (non-conscious) thought, since the resulting behaviour fitted so neatly into the practical-reasoning-model of explanation; yet that perception was an epitome of non-conscious experience.[11]

We therefore need to consider how plausible it would be to maintain that chimpanzees engage in thinking that is in turn made available for the chimpanzee to think about – to maintain that chimps can think about their own thoughts. Here is about the most intelligent thing that I know of that a chimpanzee can do.[12] It can be led around a one-acre field, observing some eighteen pieces of fruit or vegetable being hidden in various places. If it is later allowed to enter the field at a different point, it can retrieve, on average, two-thirds of the food, collecting fruit before vegetables, which reflects the chimpanzee order of preference. (In contrast, if a chimp is allowed into the field without having seen where the food is hidden, only one item will be retrieved on average.)

Consider what must be true of its cognition, for a chimpanzee to be able to do this sort of thing. It must have a cognitive map of the field, on which the positions of fruit and vegetables are marked. The chimp must also be able to position itself on the map, and direct its movements accordingly. It must also be able to update the map so as to avoid returning to the same place twice. In which case, there is certainly something very like thinking going on. But is the chimp also capable of thinking about its own thinking? There is not a shred of evidence to suggest it. There is no reason to believe that chimps can reflect upon, and improve, their own patterns of thinking. For example, a chimp that visits all the fruit locations first, and then visits the vegetable locations afterwards, will waste a considerable amount of energy in walking unnecessary distances. If the chimp were really capable of thinking about its own thinking, we might expect to see sudden changes in tactic, bringing dramatic improvements of performance. (The cases famously reported by Kohler, in which chimps seem able to hit upon sudden solutions to practical problems, are only evidence of thinking, not of thinking about thinking.)[13] In the present case, we might expect a chimp to hit upon the thought that it would be better to take the shortest route around all the items of food, carrying the vegetables if necessary to be consumed later. At any rate, human beings are conspicuous for being able to improve their performance in just this sort of way, as a result of their ability to subject their own thinkings to thought and criticism.

I am suggesting that human beings are unique amongst members of the animal kingdom in possessing conscious mental states. It might be objected that this is implausible, since it makes such a sharp division between ourselves and other animals. A more attractive picture, it may be held, is that consciousness emerges gradually as one moves up the evolutionary scale. In fact, there is a sense in which this may be true that is consistent with my account. For as the cognition of higher organisms becomes increasingly more sophisticated, and their conceptual repertoires increasingly diverse, so there will be a wider range of thoughts available for them to think. There will then be more things that they can be conscious *of*. Nevertheless, while the higher mammals display increasing degrees of awareness of properties and events in the world, it may still be that their mental states are non-conscious ones.

It is a further advantage of my account, indeed, that it makes it easy to see how consciousness might have evolved. In crude terms, all that would need to be grafted on to a cognitive structure with the capacity for thought would be a sort of feedback loop, giving human beings the further capacity to think about their own processes of thinking. Such an addition would surely have given immediate advantages in survival, since it would have conferred on us an indefinitely improvable problem-solving ability, as we noted above. It may be, indeed, that it was the fact that we evolved an innate language faculty that proved decisive in this respect. For besides extending the range of thoughts available to us, as we suggested in Chapter 6, this would have brought with it the conceptual apparatus for thinking about thoughts – the concepts, namely, of quotation, assertability, reference, and truth. If our capacity for natural language turns out to be implicated in our capacity for conscious thought, then it will be easy to see, in natural terms, how our capacity for conscious mental states might have evolved, and why that capacity should in fact be unique.

NON-CONSCIOUS PAIN

It goes without saying that pains, too, are experiences. Then two questions remain. First, does pain, like any other mental state, admit of a distinction between conscious and non-conscious varieties? If so, then the pains of all animals will be non-conscious ones, according to my general account of this distinction. Second, are non-conscious pains an appropriate object of sympathy and moral concern? If not, then the pains of animals will make no moral claims upon us.

There are no uncontroversial examples of non-conscious pain in humans, to parallel our everyday examples of non-conscious visual experience. There is an obvious reason for this, since part of the function of pain is to intrude upon consciousness, in order that we may give our full attention to taking avoiding action. But possible examples come from cases where someone is concentrating very intently upon a task, and later reports having felt no pain on injury, but nevertheless displays aversive behaviour. Suppose that Samuel is a soldier in the midst of battle, who is too caught up in the fighting to notice any pain when he badly burns his hand on the red-hot barrel of a gun. But an observer can see him jerk his hand away and nurse it in the manner characteristic of someone in pain. Should we feel sympathy in such a case? Clearly we would be sympathetic for Samuel's injury, but not for his suffering, since he felt no pain, in fact. This sort of example is incapable of carrying any great weight, however, because the pain-behaviour displayed is hardly paradigmatic. Since the episode is so brief and unstructured, it may perhaps be regarded as a mere reflex, rather than as a genuine instance of non-conscious pain perception.

Can there be cases of pain parallel to those of blindsight? That is, cases where the full (or nearly full) range of pain-behaviour is displayed, but in which the subject is not conscious of any pain? So far as I am aware, no such cases have actually occurred. But the neurophysiology of pain-perception suggests that they are in principle possible.[14] Pain in humans is mediated through two types of nerve, which generate distinct projections in the brain subserving distinct functions. Very roughly, the 'new path' is fast, is projected into the higher centres of the brain, and is responsible for precise pain location and fine discriminations of feel. The 'old path', in contrast, is slow, is projected primarily to the more ancient limbic system of the brain, and gives rise to aversion (the desire for the pain to cease). Some types of morphine can suppress the activity of the old path, while leaving the new path fully functioning. Patients report that their pain is still just as intense (it feels the same), but that it no longer bothers them (they no longer want it to stop). It seems unlikely, in contrast, that there will be any drug, or any naturally occurring lesions, that suppress the activity of the new path while leaving the old path functioning. For unlike the case of vision, the nerves of the new path have no specialised projection-area in the higher cortex, but seem rather to be mapped in a complex way into many different regions throughout it.[15] This suggests that phenomena similar to blindsight could only occur as a result of direct surgical intervention. But they do seem to be possible in principle.

Let us then imagine a case for pain similar to that of blindsight. Suppose that a particular subject, Penelope, is never conscious of any pains in her legs. But when she suffers injury in that region she displays much of normal pain-behaviour. If we jab pins into her feet, she tries very hard to make us stop, she grimaces and groans, and severe damage causes her to scream. But she sincerely declares that she feels nothing. Perhaps she initially found her own behaviour disquieting, but now she understands its basis and merely finds it a nuisance. When she twists her ankle, she does not ask for something to alleviate the pain (she says she feels none), but for something to help her relax, and to stop her from grinding her teeth and limping when she walks.

This case is clearly an imaginable one. It is a possible example (physically possible as well as logically so) of non-conscious pain – that is, of events that otherwise occupy the normal causal role of pain, but which are not available to be thought about consciously and spontaneously by the subject. In fact it is not quite correct to say that the events in Penelope occupy the normal causal role of pain. For one normal effect of pain is to give rise to a conscious desire that the pain should cease, whereas I am supposing Penelope's avoidance behaviour to be motivated by desires that are themselves non-conscious. But this will make little difference for our purposes, since if the arguments above are sound, all the desires of animals will be equally non-conscious.

It seems that pain, like all other mental states, admits of both conscious and non-conscious varieties. And then our account of this distinction will be given, as before, in terms of the availability of conscious pain to conscious thinking. In which case, if animals are incapable of thinking about their own acts of thinking, then their pains must all be non-conscious ones.

OBJECTS OF CONCERN

Ought we to feel sympathy for Penelope, in the example above? We should perhaps feel sympathy for her general condition, since it is in many ways a disturbing situation to find oneself in. But we should not feel sympathy on specific occasions of injury, since it is clear that she does not consciously suffer. Sympathy ought surely to be grounded in an imaginative grasp of what things must be like, on the inside, for the person (or animal) in question. But if the arguments above are sound, and there is nothing that it is like to be the subject of a non-conscious pain, then in Penelope's case there is nothing there to be imagined.

Not being conscious of any pain, her mental state is not an appropriate object of moral concern.

To see this clearly, suppose that you are a doctor who knows the details of Penelope's condition, and that you happen to be on the scene of an accident in which her legs have been badly injured. A number of other people are obviously injured and in pain, but Penelope is screaming the loudest. Ought you to treat her first? Clearly not, other things being equal (provided that she is not bleeding badly, for example). It would be very difficult for you to resist helping her, of course. For feelings of sympathy seem to be induced more by overt perception of pain-behaviour, than by any theoretical belief in the underlying quality of the pain. Indeed, such feelings seem likely to be fairly robust, continuing to co-exist alongside a belief that the behaviour in question is *not* caused by any conscious pain. It would, nevertheless, be moral weakness in you to treat Penelope first. For you know that her sufferings are not conscious, whereas the sufferings of the others are. Similarly, then, in the case of animals – since their pains are non-conscious, they make no real claims upon our sympathy.

While Penelope's pains are not appropriate objects of moral concern, her injury itself might be, because of its further effects upon her life, and hence on her conscious desires and disappointments. There are many things that you cannot do with badly injured legs, even if you feel no pain. As a result of her injury, Penelope may be confined to a wheelchair for some months. This will involve her in much inconvenience in the course of her daily life, and will force her to defer her long-dreamed-of skiing holiday. It is appropriate that we should feel sympathy for these things.

However, recall that on my proposed account of the distinctive nature of conscious mental states the desires of animals, as well as their experiences, will be non-conscious. If it were to turn out that non-conscious desires, like the non-conscious pains we have just been considering, are not appropriate objects of sympathy, then the injuries of animals will not even have further effects on their lives that are of moral concern. On my account, the disappointments caused to a dog through possession of a broken leg, as well as its immediate pains, are themselves non-conscious in their turn. In which case it follows that if they, too, are not appropriate objects of our sympathy, then neither the pain of the broken leg itself, nor its further effects upon the life of the dog, will have any rational claim on our sympathy.

Recall how I argued in Chapter 4 that sympathy is only appropriate for subjective, as opposed to objective, frustrations of desire. I claimed that by rebuilding the damaged statue representing Astrid's, the astronaut's, late husband I would not be acting benevolently towards her, since she would never be aware of what I had done. While such an action would prevent one of Astrid's desires from being objectively dissatisfied, she would in any case continue to *feel* that her desire was satisfied, and this is what matters. Similar considerations can be used to show that sympathy is only really appropriate for the (subjective) frustration of conscious, as opposed to non-conscious, desires. The frustration of a non-conscious desire is not something that can cause any conscious distress to the desiring subject, precisely because it is non-conscious. Equally, the satisfaction of such a desire cannot illuminate the conscious life of the one whose desire it is, again because it is non-conscious. There is, therefore, no such thing as imagining what it is like to be in the position of the desiring subject, in these respects, and the desires in question will make no rational claims on our sympathy. Then so, too, in the case of the desires of animals.

ETHICAL IMPLICATIONS

What emerges, if the considerations above are sound, is that the arguments of Regan and Singer for extending the principle of equal consideration of interests to animals, which we examined at length in earlier chapters, were in any case founded on a false premiss. For both assume that animal desires and animal experiences are relevantly similar to our own – in particular, that they are conscious ones. Recall that I argued against Regan in Chapter 1 that his attempt to ascribe intrinsic value to animals seemed to involve an unacceptable intuitionism, committing him to the view that values form part of the fabric of the world independently of us. And I argued against Singer in Chapters 3 and 4 that his utilitarianism commits him to claims about the moral standing of animals that are far too extreme to be believable. But we now have to hand an argument against both that is even more direct and decisive. For if it has been shown that the mental states of animals are non-conscious, then they cannot be appropriate objects of moral concern.

The ideas presented in this chapter would also undermine the contractualist account of our duties towards animals defended in Chapter 7. For if animal pains and dissatisfactions are not appropriate objects of sympathy, then no cruelty need be displayed in one who fails to take them seriously. In fact, the remarks made in Chapter 3 about children's supposedly cruel treatment of insects would extend to all animals. If insects are not genuinely sentient, then brutish cruelty need not be displayed in one who causes them damage. But then so, too, if the experiences of birds and mammals are non-conscious – those who discount their experiences, in consequence, need not be brutishly cruel. In the case of all those people who remain unconvinced by my arguments, of course, the position remains as it was. Anyone who continues to believe that animal pains are relevantly similar to our own will (in our culture, at least) display cruelty in causing an animal to suffer for no good reason. But if my views became widely accepted then all psychological connections between our attitudes to human and animal suffering would soon be decisively broken.

If I am right, indeed, then it ought to be strictly impossible to feel sympathy for animals, once the true nature of their mental lives is properly understood. Utilitarians are fond of claiming that if we were perfectly rational we should be equally sympathetic for the sufferings of animals as for the sufferings of ourselves. The truth may be that it is only our imperfect rationality that enables us to feel sympathy for animals at all.

I would urge caution, however. The views presented in this chapter are controversial and speculative, and may well turn out to be mistaken. Until something like a consensus emerges, amongst philosophers and psychologists concerning the nature of consciousness, and amongst ethologists over the cognitive powers of animals, it may be wiser to continue to respond to animals as if their mental states were conscious ones. This is not a concession to philosophical scepticism, just a realistic assessment of the likelihood of swift success in intellectual domains as complex and intractable as these.

SUMMARY

Mental states admit of a distinction between conscious and non-conscious varieties that is best accounted for as the difference between states that are, and states that are not, regularly made available to conscious (reflexive) thinking. Then since there is no reason to believe that any animals are capable of thinking about their own thinkings in this way, none of their mental states will be conscious ones. If this account were acceptable, it would follow almost immediately that animals can make no moral claims on us. For non-conscious mental states are not appropriate objects of moral concern.

Conclusion

It is time to pull together the threads of my argument, and briefly to set out my conclusions. In doing this I shall by-pass the position defended in Chapter 8, that the mental states of animals are non-conscious ones. For this is, at the moment, too highly speculative to serve as a secure basis for moral practice. The contents of that chapter may best be regarded as suggestions for further research.

My main argument against the moral standing of animals is that some version of contractualism provides us with the most acceptable framework for moral theory, and that from such a perspective animals must fail to be accorded direct rights, through failing to qualify as rational agents. While contractualism allows that we do have duties towards animals, these only arise indirectly – on the one hand, out of respect for the feelings of animal lovers, and on the other hand, through the good or bad qualities of character that animals may evoke in us. Most importantly, this position is not undermined by failure to accord direct rights to those human beings who are not rational agents, since such rights are in fact granted through a version of slippery slope argument, as well as through an argument from social stability.

There only appear to be two real competitors to the contractualist line on animals rehearsed above. The first is the rights-based approach of Tom Regan. But there is no way in which this can achieve reflective equilibrium, largely because of its failure to provide an adequate governing conception of the sources of morality and moral motivation. We can set Regan a dilemma, indeed. The most natural reading of his work involves him in a commitment to moral intuitionism, maintaining that moral values form part of the fabric of the world independent of our minds. While this provides us with a kind of governing conception, it is an unacceptable one, as we saw in Chapter 1. It makes a complete mystery, both of the subject-matter of morality, and of our supposed knowledge of moral truths. On the other hand, it might be possible to read Regan more neutrally, supposing that his intention is merely to pull together our common-sense moral beliefs into a coherent set of principles. Taken like this, his work provides us with no governing conception at all. But this is both unacceptable in itself and serves also to undermine many of Regan's own arguments, in so far as they depend upon claims about moral relevance, as many of them do. For as we saw in Chapter 3, relevance is always relative to some point of view, and on this reading of Regan the moral point of view would remain uncharacterised.

The other main competitor to my contractualist account is the utilitarian approach defended by Peter Singer. There are a number of reasons for preferring contractualism to utilitarianism as a framework for moral theory, as we saw in Chapter 2. But the main argument against Singer is that, when properly worked out, utilitarianism entails a position on the animals issue that is far too extreme to be taken seriously. For it is obliged to count animal suffering and animal lives as equal in standing to our own, as we saw in Chapters 3 and 4. Yet we find it intuitively abhorrent that the lives or sufferings of animals should be weighed against the lives or sufferings of human beings. Note that this argument against Singer is partially dependent upon the success of my attempt, in Chapters 5 and 7, to work out a plausible contractualist approach to the animals issue. For we can be more convincing in resisting the claim that theoretical considerations should be allowed to override our common-sense beliefs, if we have some alternative approach to offer. The dependence is only partial, however. For the beliefs in question are so deeply embedded in our moral thinking that it might be more reasonable to do without any theory of morality at all, than to accept one that would accord animals equal moral standing with ourselves. (Compare the fact that it may, in the same way, be more reasonable for us to do without a theory of knowledge at all, than to accept one that would entail that we have no knowledge of the physical world.)

The most important practical conclusion of this book is that there is no basis for extending moral protection to animals beyond that which is already provided. In particular, there are no good moral grounds for forbidding hunting, factory farming, or laboratory testing on animals. The argument for this conclusion may be summarised as follows. As claimed above, some version of contractualism provides us with the most acceptable framework for moral theory, and from such a perspective animals will be denied moral standing. There are then only two possible indirect reasons for outlawing the sorts of activities listed above. One pertains to the qualities of moral character revealed in their practitioners. But these may be insignificant, in the light of the ready psychological separability of attitudes to animal and to human suffering. The other turns on the likely offence caused to animal lovers. But this, too, fails, because of the moral costs that would accompany further extending and encouraging feelings of sympathy for animals. These feelings serve only to divert attention from the claims of those who do have moral standing, namely human beings. And no doubt in many instances they are, in any case, partly dependent upon a false belief in the equal moral standing of animals.

This is not to say, of course, that there is anything wrong with admiring animals, or enjoying their company. Nor is it to deny that there are powerful moral reasons for wishing to preserve endangered species of animal, similar to, but considerably more powerful than, the reasons for preserving great works of art. But what it does mean, is that those who are committed to any aspect of the animal rights movement are thoroughly misguided.

Notes

I MORAL ARGUMENT AND MORAL THEORY

1 Stephen Clark seems to have taken this advice to heart in *The Moral Status of Animals* (Oxford University Press, 1977), though without necessarily endorsing strong subjectivism.
2 *A Theory of Justice* (Oxford University Press, 1972).
3 For further discussion see my *Human Knowledge and Human Nature* (Oxford University Press, 1992), chs. 1 and 11–12. See also Laurence Bonjour, *The Structure of Empirical Knowledge* (Harvard University Press, 1985), and Keith Lehrer, *Theory of Knowledge* (Routledge, 1990).
4 See Tom Regan, *The Case for Animal Rights* (Routledge, 1984), pp. 324–5, and Peter Singer, *Practical Ethics* (Cambridge University Press, 1979), pp. 88–90.
5 For a dispassionate assessment of the strengths and weaknesses of arguments for the existence of God, see John Mackie, *The Miracle of Theism* (Oxford University Press, 1982).
6 Cambridge University Press, 1903.
7 For sophisticated defence of a view of this sort, see Vinit Haksar, *Equality, Liberty, and Perfectionism* (Oxford University Press, 1979).
8 See John Mackie, *Ethics* (Penguin, 1977), ch. 1.9.
9 See particularly *The Case for Animal Rights*.
10 See *The Case for Animal Rights*, ch. 7. I shall return in Chapter 5 to consider the way in which Regan attempts to extend moral standing to human babies aged less than one.

2 UTILITARIANISM AND CONTRACTUALISM

1 A charge pressed forcefully by Jack Smart in the book jointly written with Bernard Williams, *Utilitarianism: For and Against* (Cambridge University Press, 1973).
2 Oxford University Press, 1981. See also his discussion of the

utilitarian attitude towards slavery in his contribution to Peter Singer, ed., *Applied Ethics* (Oxford University Press, 1986).

3 See Michael Slote, 'Satisficing Consequentialism' in his *Common-Sense Morality and Consequentialism* (Routledge, 1985).

4 Such a view has been defended by Singer, *Practical Ethics*, ch. 8.

5 See his *Two Treatises on Government* (1690).

6 See his *Leviathan* (1651).

7 See especially his *Groundwork to a Metaphysic of Morals* (1785).

8 See his 'Contractualism and Utilitarianism' in A. Sen and B. Williams, eds., *Utilitarianism and Beyond* (Cambridge University Press, 1982).

9 See his *Groundwork to a Metaphysic of Morals*, ch. 2.

10 But for a contrary view, see Onora O'Neill, *Constructions of Reason* (Cambridge University Press, 1990).

11 Taken from his *Practical Ethics* (Cambridge University Press, 1979), ch. 8.

12 See his papers 'Justice as Fairness: Political not Metaphysical' and 'The Priority of Right and Ideas of the Good' in *Philosophy and Public Affairs* 14 (1985) and 17 (1988) respectively.

13 See 'Contractualism and Utilitarianism', pp. 116–17.

14 See my *Human Knowledge and Human Nature*, chs. 6–8.

15 See my *Human Knowledge and Human Nature*, ch. 6.

16 This is my preferred mode of defending the coherentist conception of knowledge, mentioned briefly in Chapter 1 above. I claim that it is an innate constitutive part of human reason that the justification for a belief consists, in part, in its coherence with surrounding beliefs. See my *Human Knowledge and Human Nature*, ch. 12.

17 See the two recent papers cited earlier.

18 See Michael Sandel, *Liberalism and the Limits of Justice* (Cambridge University Press, 1982).

19 'Contractualism and Utilitarianism', p. 112.

3 UTILITARIANISM AND ANIMAL SUFFERING

1 Jonathan Cape, 1975; 2nd edition, 1990.

2 See *Practical Ethics*, ch. 3.

3 For Singer's commitment to this characterisation of the moral point of view, see *Practical Ethics*, ch. 1.

4 See *The Case for Animal Rights*, ch. 5 and p. 261.

5 See H. Rachlin, *Behaviour and Learning* (Freeman, 1976), pp. 125–6.

6 See *The Case for Animal Rights*, p. 197.

7 See Stephen Walker, *Animal Thought* (Routledge, 1983), chs. 4 and 5.

8 See Walker, *Animal Thought*, ch. 6.

9 For a recent example, see Peter Harrison, 'Do Animals Feel Pain?' *Philosophy* 66 (1991).

10 See my *Introducing Persons* (Routledge, 1986), chs. 2–3 and 5, and also Peter Smith and O. R. Jones, *The Philosophy of Mind* (Cambridge University Press, 1986), Part I.

11 See my *Introducing Persons*, ch. 7.

12 For example, see my *Introducing Persons*, chs. 1 and 4–6.

13 See *Practical Ethics*, p. 52.

14 See *Practical Ethics*, p. 59.

15 See my *Human Knowledge and Human Nature*, chs. 11–12.

16 Most of those who employ the higher/lower distinction would put the pleasures of sex in general on the 'lower' side of the divide. This is a definite mistake. Normal human sex has an irreducibly intellectual component. For I do not just enjoy my own sensations (as I do when masturbating) – I am also aware that my partner is enjoying hers, and that she is similarly aware of, and takes further pleasure in, the fact that I am enjoying mine; and I enjoy that, too. In fact, there is nothing *animal* about human sex; it is a matter of mutual enjoyment in the fullest sense. In this much I follow Thomas Nagel, 'Sexual Perversion', in his *Mortal Questions* (Cambridge University Press, 1979).

17 See Aristotle, *Ethics* (*c.* 330 BC), Book 2, final section.

4 UTILITARIANISM AND THE HARM OF KILLING

1 For further discussion of the issue, see my *Introducing Persons*, chs. 3 and 7.

2 See particularly Thomas Nagel, 'Death', in his *Mortal Questions*.

3 Similar points are made by Joel Feinberg, 'Harm and Self-Interest' in P. Hacker and J. Raz, eds., *Law, Morality and Society* (Oxford University Press, 1977).

4 See *Practical Ethics*, ch. 4.

5 For discussion of the many puzzles involved, see Derek Parfit, *Reasons and Persons* (Oxford University Press, 1984), Part IV.

6 See *Practical Ethics*, pp. 88–90.

7 See *Animal Rights*, p. 324.

8 See *Practical Ethics*, p. 89.

9 See 'Life's Uncertain Voyage' in P. Pettit, R. Sylvan and J. Norman, eds., *Metaphysics and Morality* (Blackwell, 1987).

10 On this, see my *Introducing Persons*, ch. 8.

5 CONTRACTUALISM AND ANIMALS

1 See *The Case for Animal Rights*, ch. 5.4.

2 This is made especially clear in 'Justice as Fairness: Political not Metaphysical'.
3 See *A Theory of Justice*, section 22.
4 On this, see my *Introducing Persons*, chs. 7 and 8.
5 See *The Case for Animal Rights*, pp. 319–20.
6 See Helga Kuhse and Peter Singer, *Should the Baby Live?* (Oxford University Press, 1985), ch. 5.

6 ANIMALS AND RATIONAL AGENCY

1 Penguin, 1972.
2 See Walker, *Animal Thought*, pp. 372–4.
3 For detailed defence of this idea, see my *Human Knowledge and Human Nature*, ch. 8.
4 See Henry Wellman, *The Child's Theory of the Mind* (MIT Press, 1990).
5 See R. Byrne and A. Whiten, eds., *Machiavellian Intelligence* (Oxford University Press, 1988).
6 See Susan Carey, *Conceptual Change in Childhood* (MIT Press, 1985).
7 Many of these are detailed in R. G. Frey, *Interests and Rights* (Oxford University Press, 1980), chs. 7–9.
8 See 'Thought and Talk' in his *Inquiries into Truth and Interpretation* (Oxford University Press, 1984), and 'Rational Animals' in E. LePore and B. McLaughlin, eds., *Actions and Events* (Blackwell, 1985).
9 See my *Human Knowledge and Human Nature*, ch. 8.
10 See Walker, *Animal Thought*, ch. 6.
11 See Walker, *Animal Thought*, ch. 6.
12 See Fred Dretske, *Explaining Behaviour* (MIT Press, 1988), p. 4.
13 See the papers collected in Byrne and Whiten, eds., *Machiavellian Intelligence*.
14 See Singer, *Practical Ethics*, pp. 93–5.
15 For detailed development of these points, see Walker, *Animal Thought*, ch. 9.
16 See Noam Chomsky, *Language and Problems of Knowledge* (MIT Press, 1988). See also my *Human Knowledge and Human Nature*, chs. 6–8.
17 Adapted from Robert Stalnaker, *Inquiry* (MIT Press, 1984).
18 See 'Contractualism and Utilitarianism', p. 113.
19 See *Language and Problems of Knowledge*, ch. 1.
20 See my *Human Knowledge and Human Nature*, chs. 6 and 8.

7 CONTRACTUALISM AND CHARACTER

1 This point is emphasised, from a utilitarian stand-point, by Hare in *Moral Thinking*.

2 See the lecture on duties towards animals in Kant's *Lectures on Ethics* (1775–80), published in translation by Methuen.

8 ANIMALS AND CONSCIOUS EXPERIENCE

1 This is what Nagel famously did in 'What Is It Like To Be a Bat?', *Mortal Questions*, ch. 12.

2 See Lawrence Weiskrantz, *Blindsight* (Oxford University Press, 1986).

3 For these last facts I rely upon personal communication from Anthony Marcel, Applied Psychology Unit, Cambridge.

4 See Jerry Fodor, 'Imagistic Representation' in his *The Language of Thought* (Harvester, 1975).

5 See Robert Kirk, 'Consciousness and Concepts', *Aristotelian Society Proceedings* supp. vol. 66 (1992).

6 For further criticism of Kirk's proposal, as well as further discussion supporting my own theory of consciousness to be developed later in this chapter, see my 'Consciousness and Concepts', *Aristotelian Society Proceedings* supp. vol. 66 (1992).

7 See his *A Materialist Theory of the Mind* (Routledge, 1968).

8 See 'Towards a Cognitive Theory of Consciousness', *Brainstorms* (Harvester, 1978), ch. 9.

9 See my 'Consciousness and Concepts'.

10 See my *Language, Thought, and Consciousness* (forthcoming), in which I argue that the ability to use a natural language is a naturally necessary condition for us to entertain conscious thoughts, given the way in which human cognition is structured.

11 For yet further arguments that experiences need to be present to conscious (reflexive) thought in order to count as conscious, see my 'Consciousness and Concepts'.

12 See Walker, *Animal Thought*, pp. 295–6.

13 See Wolfgang Kohler, *The Mentality of Apes* (Routledge and Kegan Paul, 1925).

14 Here I rely upon the account provided by Dennett in 'Why you can't make a Computer that feels Pain', *Brainstorms*, ch. 10.

15 Here I rely upon J. Z. Young, *Philosophy and the Brain* (Oxford University Press, 1986).

Index